SELF-
IGNORANCE
IS YOUR PROBLEM.

SELF-
AWARENESS
IS YOUR SOLUTION.

SUCCESS IS YOUR BIRTHRIGHT!

LIFE IS YOURS AND

YOU ARE THE PILOT OF IT,

DO SOMETHING ABOUT IT.

notionpress.com

SELF-IGNORANCE IS YOUR PROBLEM.

SELF-AWARENESS IS YOUR SOLUTION.

SUCCESS IS OUR BIRTHRIGHT!
LIFE IS YOURS AND
YOU ARE THE PILOT OF IT,
DO SOMETHING ABOUT IT.

BENJAMIN M. OTHMAR
DEEPAK BURFIWALA

notionpress
.com

Notion Press

Old No. 38, New No. 6

McNichols Road, Chetpet

Chennai - 600 031

First Published by Notion Press 2016

ISBN 978-93-86009-05-0

Dedication

Dedicated to my readers and entire humanity. We respect you and wish you all a life full of love, peace, prosperity, wisdom, wealth, health and self-awareness.

Contents

Acknowledgments

Deepak Burfiwala

With love and respect from the bottom of my heart, I pay sincere thanks to each and every person who have directly or indirectly helped me in this life-changing journey of becoming a passionate motivational speaker and to help people find their inner voice. Let me start with all my life-changing gurus–Dale Carnegie, Shiv Khera, Peter Drucker, Mahatma Gandhi, Swami Vivekananda, Robin Sharma, Osho along with my mentors Deepak Chopra, Eminem, Emerson, Pitbull, Anthony Robbins, Saint Kabir, Briantracy, Usain Bolt, Henry Ford, Wayne Dyer, Aamir Khan, Lady Gaga and Amitabh Bachchan, who are responsible for the divine realization of my inner potential in my life. My heartfelt salute to my grandparents and my parents, sister and brother-in-law for being so kind to me every time. Our children, Vanshika and Aaravare, have also proved to be great motivators in this journey. My uncles, Mr Krishan Chand, Mr Mahesh Chand, Mr Suresh Chand and Mr Prakash, are very kind and respectful to me. My life partner, Seema Burfiwala, who is a pure soul mate and an unconditional friend, is a key person in my life and it is because of her trust in my writing skills I have earned the courage to write such stuff. My brother-cum-soul mate, Sandeep Jangra, who is a passionate entrepreneur, has always been a source of inspiration for me. His style of working and listening to new ideas is just awesome.

My visionary friends, Deepak Sharma, Ajay Godara, Navdeep Vishnuvanshi, Jasbir Pahuja, Kamal Rana, Sunil

Kumar, Ravinder Singh, Sandeep Boora, Satinder Singh, Jagtar Singh, Deepak Rangurangu, Manohar Mehra, Mohit Sharma, Vikram Sharma, Dhruv Sharma, Ankul, Gaurav Agarwal, Amit and Sumit (Jangra Brothers), Jaideep Kharb, Sandeep Teka, Sachin Bodla, Parul Mittal, Shivanshu Arora, Parmod Rohilla, Trilok Bajwa, Dilbagh Mehla, Rajneesh Choudhary, Ravi Kirpal, Jaganjeet Gill, Dishant Chopra, Mandeep Punia, Sanjay Kaushik, Kailash Chawla, Krishankant Sharma, Manish Gupta and Yogesh Jangra deserve a grand thanks for supporting me with their precious blessings and support.

My sincere thanks to all the platforms that fortunately I have received in my life ranging from DCRUST Murthal, Sonipat to DCM, Shreeram Consolidated Limited to Austenitic Creations Private Limited, Technology Education Research Integrated Institutions, Kurukshetra to LLS24 to Millennium Career Consultants where I worked, learned and evolved. More than 500+ schools (all over Haryana) and their 50,000+ eager students taught me how to be humble and inspirational on the stage. More than 100+ professional institutes training sessions in which I learnt awesome lessons of training people for permanent impact were worthy experiences of my life journey. I am honestly thankful to all these schools and institutes.

My first publisher Pigeon Books led by Mr Kaushal Goyal, an amazing person who has shown faith in me and made me a published author in March, 2012, is also an important part of my life. Whatever I've become as an author today is because of his faith and humble guidance. May god bless him and all his loved ones.

Great personalities like Dr M P Gupta, Dr L N Mittal, Dr K L Johar, Dr A S Choudhary, Dr Dimple Juneja, Dr Sukhwinder

Singh, Mr Ved Prakash, Mr Jasbir Khatkar, Dr Mukesh Arya, Mr Khuhsi Ram, Mr Surender Dhull, Mr Jaswinder Pabnawa, Mr Vimal Sareen, Dr Parmod Mahajan, Mr Sanjeev Sehgal, Mr Kapil Chaudhary, Mr Radheyshyam Jangra, Mr Surender Singh, Mr Vijay Jangra and Mr Sukhbir Jangra are very helpful and blessings of my life. I give my sincere thanks to Success Monks Organization, founded by Siddhartha Sharma, an international success coach and author, for opening me towards my inner talents and inspired me to follow my heart.

Benjamin M Othmar

Thanks to the almighty God for offering me another opportunity to live and all those whom he used in the course of my life and my family at large. First I would like to thank my brother Othmar Wurth and M Stefan whose simple, pure love, guidance, encouragement, affection, inspiration and advices have always encouraged me to fulfill my dreams. I don't know where I would be without you – "without you there would be no life changing to Ben, May Lord Bless You. Special thanks to my mum Ange Condo Umutoni for your unending love and support you have given to me over the years.

I would like to thank the great family of Hazitamungu Theodomile, for their support they have given to me over the years. Thanks to Bishop Kayinamura Samuel, Rev Paster Eraste Ndacyekwa, Paster Foustin Niyindengera, Jeanine Condo, Chantal Condo, Hakizimana Gilbert, Rwanyonga, Papa Obe, Nina Condo, Barutwanayo Jean Gilbert, Dr Karambizi, Prof Keffa, Prof Byarugaba, Dr Kibuka, Dr Mwaniki, Dr Isac Abuga, Mutuyeyezu Osward, Lazale Ndazale, Nyiraneza, Vincent Konadu, Mwumvaneza John

Ladislaus, Haguma Appolinaire, Dr Rutebuka Balinda, Ndagije Mukasine Esta, Theoneste Gasangwa and Rugabisha Thomas for your advices, opinions, ideas and support on way to great smile. I would like to extend my gratitude to all our teachers in Rwanda, Uganda (Africa) and in India for that I have learnt, they have encouraged me and put up with my commitment. Special thanks to Prof Ruhul Gupta Jain-, Director of International Affairs, MM University (MMU), Mullana, Dr Harish Sharma, Director of International Affairs, Dr Anil Chandok, Ranjit, Director of NIIT Ambala, Gourav Kalra, Ms Rashmi Garg Country Coordinator (MMU), Mr Naveen, Account Branch (MMU), Rishi Dhiman,Sarabjit Singh Shergill Ass Professor & Head PIET School of Management and Technology, Joseph Kabakeza First Counsellor High Commission of the Republic of Rwanda, New Delhi, Saud Mansoor, Founder of Ispeedread Bangalore, Dr Sakshi Sharma (Ass Professor, MMIM), Dr Balwinder Kaur (Associate Professor, MMIM) for your kind words and teaching – you have been a source of knowledge and inspiration, you have made my vision to become a reality.

Dr P SVohra, Principal (MMIM, Mullana, Ambala, India) is an international motivational and personal empowerment speaker, whose teaching and advices inspired me to become successful as a person. Thanks to Umubyeyi Vestine whose editorial patience, skills and recommendations made this a better book. Thanks to Kigabiro Aymard who believed in me and encouraged me in different ways. To Ndikuyera Robert who worked through each of the sentences and made many invaluable, contributions.

Vanita Dua, Peeyush Ranga, Priyanka Ranga, Rahul Mehra, Pradeep, Ndayiragije Armard Pacific, Sunny Singh,

Anik, Umuhomaziwabo Marie Alice, Emmy Arsonval Maniriho, Huguette, Parampreet, Uwamahoro Edith, Mushikiwabo Sarah, Usman Umar Zango, Bahaa Denio, Sadiq Abdullah Waziri – thanks to you all for your well wishes, encouragement, cooperation and being there for me in the time of need when I was in campus and PGI Hospital, India.

I therefore extend my deep and special thanks to Dr M L Ranga, Vice Chancellor of Guru Jambheshwar University of Science and Technology, University of Hisar, Haryana, India for providing everything needed to meet with ENT specialist Dr Reeju Neetaat at PGI. Thanks to all my friends in MMU and Member of Christian Student Fellowship, Mullana, Ambala your enthusiasm, commitment and camaraderie, you are special peoples to me. Thanks to Apotre Gitwaza, Paul of Zion Temple Church who gave me special Prayers in 2005, may God bless you. Special thanks to all members of Children Help Network (CHN) in Europe who sponsored me for all my levels of education. I don't know where I would be without you, without your support – Ben's life would be in darkness–may God bless you.

Last but not the least, a big special thanks to Notion Press for improving, designing and publishing this book.

What this Book is About

Have you ever been in a desperate situation? Have you ever lost hope? Have you ever not known what to do with your future? Have you failed in business, class and relationships? Have you asked yourself what are your talents and gifts? Have you asked yourself, why some people are so much successful in their life but others are not? What is the difference between these people? Have you ever needed support without success? If you have experienced one of these, and it happens that you are reading this book, you are a great achiever. In the journey of life, it is not guaranteed that you will walk through smoothly paved paths. At times, you have to tread over holes and stones.

But when you let yourself go with self-ignorance, you will certainly fall into the hole or hit a stone. The same thing will happen if you get distracted by unnecessary movements in the same path. By only controlling your steps and keeping in mind your destination, you will certainly reach your destination without any harm, through self-awareness.

We all know that every house or building is established based on architectural plans or drawings. Every architect first formulates the plan or picture of the house in mind, through imagination, before drawing it on paper. You are the architect of your future and life. Whether your future is of prosperity or misery; it will all come from within you, from the functioning of your mind. Self-awareness will be a key aspect in all your future achievements and fulfillments.

Some people like to say that life is hard; but today we say that life is only hard when you let its difficulties get over its opportunities. Your future is easy to make when you go with self-awareness, but it is hard when you just sit and enjoy self-ignorance and waiting for some miracles to happen. Ben had a colleague in the university, who was always in trouble with professors because of one thing. He was always late to submit his assignments.

Ben did not understand why his colleague was always late, until he found out what was really the matter. The colleague used his personal laptop and to access the Internet, he had to use mobile internet bundles. One day, they worked together on an assignment and when done, Ben submitted his work. The next day, he heard his friend complaining about his internet bundles which ran out of currency before he submitted his work. He was then blaming the network company, that they were thieves, and that they cut his bundles unfairly. I was curious to know what really happened to him because we all know that Internet bundles are cut, depending on the time you used it to browse, or the downloads that you do. I then took his computer and had a look on what he was doing. He was reading entertainment news, football fixtures and listening to online music. He had even downloaded a short funny video. I was surprised because I could not understand how he could complain, when he misused his bundles before he could submit his work.

Life is also a kind of Internet bundle. Your success will depend on how you well manage your life. Your success will depend on how you well manage yourself by using your natural untapped talents, dormant power, hidden ability and unused strength within you. What Ben's colleague could have done was to submit his assignment first and get entertained after, or even save the remaining bundles for his next assignments. The task in life on earth and in heaven, for those who believe, is to achieve. On earth, we are in a race to live a better life, those who do not have lunch are striving to get at least the supper, those who do not have shelter are striving to get a house, those who do have houses are striving to get villas and those who drive cheaper cars are striving to get more expensive ones. We strongly believe that all of us have something we want to achieve, or to accomplish in our life time. To get there, a lot of sweat and commitment must get involved. As Philip Holden author of the book, 'Super Success' said "Don't expect that your life will always be easy. Success won't be delivered to you on a plate." The older you grow, the bigger your achievements should be.

Remember, the one who made you, packaged you with all that you need to be whatever you want to be and He gave you the authority to become whatever you want to become. He gives you will power. You are a full package of infinite creativity and infinite inner resources and you are indeed a complete power house on your own. You can use it to enhance your life and to bless the society or you can use this immense power to break your life and become a liability for your society. The choice is yours and it is your life and you are the **PILOT** of it.

This book is about how to succeed in life, business, relationships, academics and many areas of life. This is your own manual to lifelong peace, success, happiness, prosperity, self-awareness and achieving fulfillment in life. It is about how to be a better person, step by step, everyday both in your personal and professional life. By going through this life-changing eternal success manual, you can achieve accomplishment excellently and respectfully in the assignments that God has created you to do, before you die. You can live fully and die empty with the awesome insights of this book. We believe that you are born to make a positive impact on this planet. You are here to make your mark. You are here to shine as a masterpiece. You are here to discover your calling. You are here to live a life of purpose and meaning. You are on this earth, to discover your truth. You are here to become more as a person, every single day. You are full of inner infinite creative potential which is within you, since your first breath.

This book will unleash the lasting motivation, powerful ideas and qualities of many successful people around the world. Some of them are still alive planet and grace the earth with their inner beauty.. While others have died, their experiences and advice are still there to help you to achieve your inner excellence both in your personal and professional life, as it has done to us. A Chinese proverb says, "To know the road ahead, ask those coming back."

In this powerful and now, your own book, we want our esteemed and worthy readers to get motivated and understand what it takes to have big achievements, no matter who you are, no matter what you have at present in your bank account. This might sound absurd, because many of us believe that big achievements are brought by big investment of money, or having a respected name, or even being educated to the highest level. Through Ben's life experiences, he has discovered that if you think big, if you have a dream and goal, if you develop the courage to concentrate on your goals, something for sure, will happen in your life. Throughout this awesome book, we will be sharing amazing life lessons to help you in the direction of your self-awareness.

We are very much aware that life is full of surprises, positive and negative, but we strongly believe that there is nothing called luck. You create luck through your hard work for years, in the direction of your passion. It is not by chance that someone owns a car or he is living an abundant life, there is a science behind it. We call that science, self-awareness. No one is unlucky to live in misery, because there is always a way to get out from a miserable life. Remember, the holy Bible says that God would never allow temptations to come to you, when there is no way out.

Take your time and explore with us, the awesome and eternal way to unleash your inner talents. You are the only big capital needed in your achievement. You are your destiny maker. You deserve to get success. Your passion, goals and dreams are strong enough than anything else. When you begin to trust and put yourself in a situation to make it happen, you will make it happen. Make your "I can, I am able, it is possible, it can be done and yes I can," stronger than your "I can't." We have shared with you the nine easy steps of achieving abundance in your life. We believe that you have greatness within you and you have unlimited potential within you. You have something exceptional to give to this planet, which was not here before your existence. Our respectful reader the biggest failure you can have in your life is making the mistake of never trying at all.

Robin Sharma wrote in his book "The Mastery Manual" that this very day is the day that you can make a choice to stand for something higher and be the person, you know in your heart, you have always wanted to be.

We respect you because you have inner infinite creative potential within you, but you are simply not aware about it. We have given our best to make your realize that you too can become a celebrity, you too can live a life of your dreams, you too deserve to live a life of love, peace, prosperity, abundance, wisdom, wealth, health and self-awareness.

With love and respect,
Benjamin Othmar
Deepak Burfiwala

Part 1

Benjamin's Journey from Self-Ignorance to Self-Awareness

1. My Real Life Story

Let's tell you a bit about my Personal life, in the village when I grew from, there is no electricity up-to now. You need to cover so many kilometers in search of water. People fetch water from wells, valleys and hills. A majority of the population is peasants and schools or roads are scarce in the area. At six years, the school I went to remained something of an enigma to describe the classrooms were not cemented and were dusty. We would pour water on the floor, to settle the dust, so that we could concentrate on our learning. We lacked chairs too. During rains you would find rusty iron sheets leaking above our heads.

At times, someone would carry a stone into the classroom. Once, we all converged in into one classroom and were eighty from three different classes to have our lessons. We would conduct our lessons from the outside, seated on the dust, on grass and sometimes under the shade of an avocado tree. In the hot sun, we would sweat a lot and to write on our black boards seemed tacky. Exams were conducted under the shade of trees, while standing. This prolonged bare footed standing on the dust encouraged sand fleas to our feet. Shoes were mystery to us.

At the age of 5, my father breathed his last and left mother, a widow and my four sisters. She was illiterate no college training no degree. A great thank goes to the Almighty, because she loved us unconditionally. She had a good knowledge of taking care of her children. She would make all effort to pay our school fees which were worth 300 Rwanda Francs (half a dollar) in a year. To pay our school fees required her to go to dig, for our neighbors. She would be paid a wage of seventy rwf or should sometimes work for food. It was very hard to study during those times; we would get nothing to eat when our mother was tired or sick. Before going to school, I had to first fetch water with a jerry can that was heavier than I. It was my custom to arrive late to school.

When we hear a whistle in the morning, it was mandatory for everybody to go to the assembly, to sing the national anthem while raising the flag. It was a law to stop moving during such occasions. After the assembly, we would hasten for our lessons. Late comers were given a cool punishment like kneeling on the concrete ground and awaiting other punishments. The punishments included caning, cleaning the school, toilets or sometimes digging the school garden and even fetching water.

It was my custom to do all that work from Monday to Friday. Sometimes, I would miss my morning lessons, as I came in late. Sometimes, the teachers would punish me and on entering the class, other students could giggle at me. Getting lunch was also a problem. During the lunch hour, my sisters and I would go out with others playing, but on reaching home, we would only drink water and go back to school. Life was so hard to describe here.

One incident, I recall on our way from school, we found a tree which was in our compound having fallen on our house and had dismantled one part. It had rained heavily and where the tree was lying, was exactly on the stone where we could hide our keys, for easy location by family members or not to lose it. It was too big a stone and was thus difficult to lift. I looked at the stone, very hungry as a wolf, and again turned on my sisters who were also in the same plight. Really it was terribly excruciating that mother wasn't there.

"Life is really simple but we insist on making it complicated."

- CONFUCIUS

Life is easy, when you think is easy and it is simple, it is people who complicate it

If You Can't, Then Who?

The problem of a stone under a tree kept ringing in my ears and at last heard I a voice saying "If you don't do it, who will lift this stone then? If you can't, then who?" I immediately told my elder sister to look for the ways of how we can get rid of the tree, so as to get the key because there wasn't any other choice.

That is how some people at times, meet challenges and give them the place to be a burden without taking any action. There is only one key question, *"if you can't then who?" answer that question.* There was a Panga (a broad heavy knife used in Africa) in the compound which I would use when clearing or cutting grasses for animals. I picked it and started cutting until I finished the branches, while my sister was pulling them to the side. After cutting the branches, we started cutting the trees in portions so as to be able to drag it aside to get the key. I pulled and pulled but all in vain. I doubled my efforts and luckily enough I saw the log falling which was pressing against the stone.

I was over joyed because I had accomplished my task. But there was again another struggle. The stone had sunk deep in the ground due to the weight of the tree. The only method to pull it was to dig around it. I quickly got a hoe and dug it until I was able to pull it out. At last we picked the key to open the door and entered the house. The tree had destroyed one part because our house was built temporarily with mud and timber.

We started digging out the soil, but indeed the roofing had broken to pieces. As dusk fell, my mother came home from her. She was terribly shocked and asked the whole story about what had happened. It was not until we finished narrating the incident, when tears started gathering in her eyes. After a few minutes, my mother exclaimed, "let's endure, there is nothing we can do, what happened has happened." She ordered us to go for domestic work.

2. My Big Dream to Become a PhD Holder

"Whatever the mind of man can conceive and believe, it can achieve."

- NAPOLEON HILL

"We become what we think about."

- EARL NIGHTINGALE

"If you can dream it, you can achieve it."

- ZIG ZIGLAR

In our village there was a neighbor who had a relative in Kigali. He was a PhD holder and was lecturing in our national university. I remember him coming to visit us with children who were nice looking in shoes and expensive attires. Whenever they came to the village, everybody realized their presence. My mother had wished me to work hard and become like him and indeed that was also my passion.

One evening, came a woman, a friend of my mother and told her, "Do you know what?" I have seen the doctor...he has come, I saw hooting cars! "It's up to them," my mother replied. Won't the rain shower my children? Will they stop suffering? My son is not yet grown up; perhaps if he grows up, he shall also be a doctor and free me from this persistent poverty. I was splitting firewood, when I heard the news of the arrival of the doctor. Seeing the grief my mum was in, the vision she had in me, and being the second time hearing that, I started shedding tears. I stopped splitting firewood instantly. Upset, I hastened into the room. Reaching there, I said, whatever the cost, I must be a doctor and relieve mum from all those burdens she suffers for us." That was the source of all my dreams about being a doctor and makes life different by helping my mum, even building a reasonable house, different from what we were in. We took shelter in that dismantled house which was covered with floods and was too cold. The mattress I used to sleep on had even rotted. 3 rooms of our house had been destroyed. We covered the openings with banana leaves and fibers to see if the night could pass!

You can imagine the dream of a doctor coming from such a poverty stricken family. The other women who were spreading unfruitful gospel went as light was giving a place to darkness. As food was ready, we washed our hands and we were welcomed on the table with two neighboring friends. As we were eating, my sisters and others started a conversation. To me things were different. I was as silent as a grave, reflecting upon what had passed that day.

Finally, I came to a conclusion and exclaimed, "Mum, I must be like that man who has come, and wish to build for you a different house, not like this one." Before I finish those words, I was cut short by the giggles of my sisters and other children, telling me with much sarcasm, "Sincerely don't you know that in our family, **we don't have any educated person. You will be a doctor, where?** You who is always dodging, failing, and whom all other students call a fool you will be a doctor, stop throwing dust into our eyes. They all ambushed me. My mum then intervened and stopped them from laughing at me."

("Leave my son! He will achieve his goals! If others can, why not he? His dreams will come true. My Mum said emphatically "Hear my son, you are now growing because you seem to have mature plans. To want is to be able, be a devil; you will make it, be disciplined, have love, and respect for others and don't stop dreaming." Ben, always have dreams. But above all, in whatever you do, choose only what gives your future, hope, peace and happiness for you and for others. May you prosper, my son, God bless your dreams and goals." *As Napoleon Hill said that, "The No. 1 reason people fail in life is because they listen to their friends, family, and neighboring."*

I felt assimilating those words of wisdom from my mother. These words renewed my hope. Desires started haunting me, I felt wanting to build a permanent house for mum, not to see her mingling in the mud. Felt changing the life style we were in, and relieve mum from working for others. I started seeing things in another direction. Before going to sleep, my mum, as her custom was, brought a copy of the Bible and read for us, from the book of Mathew 7: 7

"Ask it shall be given you," and that became my daily prayer. I got a pen and noted the chapter and verse on a paper and kept reading those words morning and evening. She loved me so much and wanted me to be successful in life, to be a useful person to her and to society, at large. But above all, she wanted me to develop a disciplined mind and cultivate a spirit self-reliance that will enable me to cope with the future.

"The person who says it cannot be done should not interrupt the person who is doing it."

- CHINESE PROVERB

"If you don't design your own plan, chances are you'll fall into someone else's plan and guess what they have planned for you? Not much."

- JIM ROH

"Setting goals is the first step in turning the invisible into visible."

- TOM ROBBINS

"A man is the product of his thoughts; what he thinks, he becomes."

- M.K. GANDHI

"Who seeks shall find."

- SOPHOCLES

3. My Former Classroom Experience

Even though, I had those dreams of becoming a doctor, and change our lifestyle, schooling was repugnant to me. I had no interest in it at all and I hated reading books. In the school I used to go to, I was not an easy guy. I was very stubborn, fighting with others when the teacher was teaching. I used to sit at the back, making such a hullabaloo, that I hindered others from listening to the teacher. I had a good teacher who could motivate learners by asking questions. You could only put your hand up if you knew the answer. But his logic was to ask those who could not put their hands up.

I had learnt that trick and when he would ask a question. I raised my hand up, though I would be empty headed. One day, I fought with another student who had dropped my exercise book down when by passing. I was furious and I slapped him on the back who later on cried bitterly and so did I, disrupting the class which was taking notes of the teacher from the blackboard. I was seated idle, not waiting to copy notes from the blackboard even those of the previous lessons. I had missed them. The noise of the students alerted the teacher who turned and asked the one who was crying what was wrong.

The students told him that it was Ben who had slapped him at the back. He again asked me why I did so, and even though I was also shedding tears, I did not fear to tell lies, "He deliberately threw my book in the front and even beat me." All the students shouted at the top of their voices at once, "He is fooling, he is the one who has slapped him, and that is his nature, weren't you kneeling there due to failure? And behold, you are now fighting." Finally the teacher asked me "Ben, what are you doing?" I responded, "Nothing." He immediately requested me to bring my book so as to check what I had written like the others. To his amazement, he found almost nothing but only drawings. He asked me, "Ben, when others are taking notes, you are disturbing others who are interested." He got hold of my sweater around the neck, and made me kneel in the compound giving peace to other students. There was chaos, and shouts among students towards me.

I sneaked outside the school compound while others were busy taking notes. My tears started rolling down my cheeks, as a result of grief. All other students bombarded me with their laughter. The teacher called me and said Ben, "Go away from here. Reduce this noise in the class. If want to cry go home, give us peace, or else go and look after the pigs or the goats with your mother. Never come back to my class." He chased me out of the school. Upon hearing those harsh words, my tears ceased and I hoped that may be, he was going to give me mercy. It was not until that he repeated twice, that I knew that this was no joke.

When I delayed a bit, he quickly gave me my board and all my books and requested me to vamoose. I obeyed and went, making heavy steps thinking of the cock and bull story I was going to tell mum but all in vain, "What will I say?" Now I have been expelled from school, I tried to cry so as to see if he can give me mercy but there was no response. How am I going to tackle mum? 300 rwf for school fees wasted? Dreams of becoming a doctor were so finished? I was in coma! What a disgusting condition!

On my way to home, I could imagine what I was going to say about my expulsion. A terrible fear ran over my body. There are things we normally do willingly but when we suffer the consequences, we start regretting, that was my case. I thought of a trick to cry on my way home. Then I went home and found mum there. Seeing that my teacher had chased me from his class forever. "What have you done"?

I told her that the teacher posed a question and when I failed it, he punished me by making me kneel down behind, till other students finished answering the questions. Secondly, a certain student dropped my book down and I slapped him on the back and who later retaliated by slapping me also, and again I was given a punishment of kneeling down. Because of much pain, I started crying and he approached me, expelling me from his class forever. "Wipe yourself and we go together to ask him." My mum told me. There was no eating; I only took water to drink.

Reaching the school, she asked the teacher what had gone wrong and the teacher responded by raising almost 13 allegations.

- Your son is dull in class.
- He is ever shouting in class.
- He doesn't show any interest in my lessons.
- Taking notes is a sin to him.
- Ever gamboling.
- Ever last to arrive at school and first to go out before time.
- Guilty of school rules.
- Ever abusing everyone in class.
- Very lazy and good for nothing.
- He's master hand up and master head empty.
- Ever laughing jackass, disturbing others from studying.
- No respect of self-knowledge.

As that was not enough, the teacher also brought a record book of discipline and found almost remaining with few points to be given expulsion. My exercise books were again handed over to my mum who shockingly found them filled with only funny drawings. The teacher, afterwards brought another an exercise book from another student and on checking, she found it very organized, with beautiful notes. The mark sheets of the former term were also brought and I had only scored 25%.

I Decided to Change

My mum, the teacher and I were still standing and reports about my conduct kept ringing in my ears. I stared at mum and she also did the same. Out of the blue, her eyes turned watery. The one, who was everything to me, was by then shedding tears due to my rotten behavior. She called me "Ben, surely are you really the one who did all these? Before she ended talking I come closer to her, crying and get hold of her dress and painfully told her, mum, I indeed accept all, yes is me who did these mistakes. I misbehaved, but forgive me, from today; I'm going to show a difference. I'm going to change, Mum **enough is enough**!"

In front of you mum, I vow to heaven and earth that I will never fall again. I am going to start reading books and copy notes that I have missed and by the end of this week, I will show them to you. Mum, I appeal to you that I'm going to change," I beg you kindly that you forgive me." It was after a long a pause that my teacher was convinced and told mum that he had forgiven me and requested me to go back to class.

"My son, really are you going to change? My mum asked humbly with keen interest. Yes of course! Mum, am going to change," I replied with relief. There was again a moment of silence, my mum glanced at me and so did I. At last she told me, *"Never should you repeat those mistakes, I want you to become a man of integrity and successful person. God be the guide." "Oh thank you Mum," I said confidently.*

"There is no turning back; my brilliance will keep on increasing." I assured her. I entered the classroom with much *hunger of making a change and be successful by achieving my dreams.* Mum left. When the teacher entered, I requested him to change my seat from the back to the front seat and set a goal of never failing in class and be some else in my life.

- I started approaching the students we so called bright students to tell me the tricks they use to pass exams, how they revise their notes, books they read, time they wake up and went to sleep, how they plan for the exams.
- I followed the school rules and techniques the smatter students used, to be the best in class.
- I resumed the idea of taking notes.
- I started to develop the courage of reading books, visiting the library every day.
- I was always in my school uniform.
- I was always asking questions to teachers and smarter students, to know more.
- I started giving less time for football, and became more serious in my studies. I found out that the problem was me, for not using my memory effectively and all my personal potential which most of people do. They don't want to make change in their lives. But according to my experience, if you follow step by step, other successful techniques, you can achieve the same results.

"I attribute my success to this: I never gave or took any excuse."

- FLORENCE NIGHTINGALE

"The only person you are designed to become is the person you decide to be."

- RALPH WALDO EMERSON

My Mom's and My Happiness for a Big Achievement and Celebration

After changing myself by reading books, taking notes and following the semesters, it so happened that I jumped from the average of **25% to 88%.** I was the second in class, woo!!. As **Frank Sinatra** said, **"The best revenge is massive success."** Good achievement. That was great achievement. When the semester would close, they used to reward the best performers and I couldn't imagine it happening to me. As the semester was about to close, we were told to bring our parents. I brought my mum and we were seated together waiting for the results. All teachers had also assembled to thank the best performers. The ceremony commenced, by the head teacher welcoming, every one present, majorly the parents.

The teacher in charge who was the master of the ceremony called the first best student. There was a thunderous clap everywhere and that student majestically stood up and went in front to get his rewards and there after returned to his seat. Then there was another long pause every one very anxious to know who was going to be the second.

It was beyond me on hearing the teacher read my name, **"Benjamin"** and calling me in front. Astounded as I was, and the teacher holding my arm, a hullabaloo was made my class mates, before the teacher made a comment. I was terrible embarrassed and my heart missed a beat. I started thinking perhaps that he was going to reveal all my evil habits of the past to the congregation. After the noise had reduced, he said, "I would request everyone here to join me and thank Benjamin for his conduct in the second semester *The former Benjamin was very stubborn, disliked school, couldn't take notes,* *a good fighter, addicted to football, you can recall more than this. He was pig headed. He was completely hopeless in Math. But thereafter, he made a decision for the change. He promised his mum and I that he was going to be a well behaved student in the class. So ladies and gentlemen, this boy you're seeing here, had scored an average of 25% in the first semester and was the 37th out of 39 students. But now as I speak, he has scored 88% and the second out of 39 students. Assist me in thanking him."*

Before finishing, he was and whispers, everybody started clapping. All the teachers came to shake hands with me and to my amazement, students held me up! There was a commotion in the whole school because of me. I was a hero! At last, the MC requested all to keep silent, and to continue the program. A long silence followed. Then he again called me in front because students were all over me. He then said these words, "There is something special within you. For sure, congratulations, maintain the same spirit, push yourself for next level, use your imagination." Then she called mum to come to the front to pick my report form. I saw mum coming joyfully with broad smiles on her face. She held me to her bosom, affectionately, patting my back. "That's fine," she said, "only those who work hard succeed in life."

We were again given claps. She told me, "my son, thank you for having made a good reputation among all those parents." She cast a glance at me and so did I, and I remembered the time when her eyes were full of tears after my expulsion, then being replaced by happiness. "I have achieved my aim," I said heartedly.

The MC continued and said "this is the reason as to why I appeal to every student to borrow a lesson from Benjamin's attitude to change and set a goal, because after formation, there is no doubt, you become successful." It becomes painful for us teachers, whenever we see students not studying zealously.

"Congratulations Benjamin and mum don't relax, double next time, thank you so much." Seeing how joyful my teacher and mum were, I firmly decided never to fail in class until I completed all education. With my personal experience, I can therefore say that even you, yourself being alive, are a capital. There are so many talents which are bestowed in you. You can do and achieve anything you want, if you believe and trust in yourself. You need to ask yourself. What are my goals and meaning of my life? How am I striving to achieve them? Leave alone the challenges you are facing and develop a belief.

When You Change Yourself, Things Will Follow.

"Change your thoughts and you change your world."

- NORMAN VINCENT PEALE

What do I mean by this statement is that a majority of people live lives that are challenging in poverty and achieving nothing because of themselves. They fail to make a change in their lifestyle and spend their valuable time looking for reasons for their failure. In the case of students, here are some of the reasons they put forward for their poor performance in studies.

1. I didn't get enough time to prepare for my exams,
2. The exam was too hard.
3. The teacher under marked me.
4. I was late for the exam.
5. I hate the teacher of this subject.

6. I don't have potential of studying and exactly like others.
7. I was disturbed by bad weather.
8. Time became an enemy to me.
9. Mathematics and science subjects are naturally hard.
10. Didn't get enough scholastic material.

However, all these reasons are avoidable, because there are others who pass through them and yet succeed. Why can't you call them the secret of their success? *No one is smart than you, remember you are not stupid except if you're convinced yourself.* And yet others raise other reasons like I lack a certain level of education in order to start this business. I can't do this job. This job is shameful. The salary is too little I don't have good clothes like my friends. I can't start work until I find a suitable place for my career. I will go to work if time becomes conducive. I will open my business after my studies and get a lot of money. I will start if I get time. I can't do business which is not mine. I don't have friends to assist me to do this or that. I know I can't. I can't speak in public. I am sure that won't work. I know this won't work out for me. I knew I wouldn't get that job and many more. The list of excuses is long. You need to settle down and come out with strategies and accept your weaknesses, like how I did and move forward not step back, to make things happen. When you change the way you see yourself and the way you see things positively, everything will change, and your life will change forever. No excuse must be put forward to hinder us from a achieving our goals.

"Everything is practice."

- PELE

"We are what we repeatedly do."

- ARISTOTLE

"There is a great sleep within every person. When that giant awakes, miracles happen."

- FREDRICK FAUST.

"Everyone is born a king and most die in exile."

- OSCAR WILDE

4. Best Principle Practices for Your Life Plan

When you have a plan in your life, you need to put it in action and you must be prepared to do everything possible to achieve it. Here is something you need to follow:

1. Have a pen and a paper and write what you need to achieve in your life, short lived and long lived plans. Begin by saying I want to be...
2. Review your goals and dreams twice a day.
3. Plan for your goals.
4. Be assured that nothing will make you fail your goal. Ask yourself the following questions: What is needed in order to achieve my goal? What strategies are needed to achieve my goal? If you do that, something will happen.
5. Be in a position to find help from those people who have achieved the same goal as yours.
6. Try to follow their advice but have your own stand. Imitate their goal deeds but change the way you have been doing your things if not the same.
7. Instead of seeing how big the problems you will face when you begin, see how big your goal will be, when you have achieved it.

8. Be focused on your dreams and be of good qualities rather than your problems.
9. Remember that you are not what people say you are, but rather what God said you will be. People can't determine your destiny but you can determine it yourself.
10. Don't be demoralized because of what is happening to you for whatever, happens with a reason, learn from them, get experience, and use them in future.

Though That Was the End of My Dreams

Turning back to my lifetime briefly, I had reformed to a good student, but on whatever cost I have to reach somewhere. But as I have said before, many things tend to weaken us. In 1994 at nine years old. In my country was genocide against Tusti. I am not going into the details here. So, as things went wrong, we escaped to Burundi, I stayed in a refugee camp. We would eat maize soaked in water in the morning and sometimes I would stay on an empty stomach until the next day. We could cook using papyrus. So there in the camp, I didn't have any hope that my dreams would come true. I came back to my country, Rwanda in 1996. During that time, no could take care to me. I became a street boy for a long time. I would carry peoples' luggage to and from the market, to get something to eat, whereby they would beat me, and abuse me to be a thief.

I was beaten by whoever felt like beating me, using anything of his or her choice of sticks and stones. But God was on my side! No one beat me to death! That's why I'm now alive.

Praise him, for He protects His creatures and when time comes it turns problems into answers. My hospitable place was a dust bin; I could move all day long without any destination. My bed was boxes. I didn't know a mattress or shoes. Whenever it would rain, I ran at night carrying boxes on my head to get to where to sleep lavender and pass my nights. I was a cursed creature! The police could handle me as if I was a reckless bastard. I could scramble for bits of food from garbage bins. I wondered why my life had been a marathon race. I imagined whether God knew what was happening to me or whether I existed.

But I have found that God is change maker. He is ready to make our tomorrow better. In the due course of raising you, He does not consider your origin, height, beauty, tribe or anything else. He can also take you from the dust bin into a school, give you scholarship and also give you the opportunity to move to different countries seeking for knowledge abroad. God can change your situation in one second. God is good all the time. He can make a way where there is no way.

Be firm, for God always considers His own. God is above all your suffering, to turn the hard tasks into nothing and again remember that "Our suffering is the only way of achieving the best."

One day in 1997, I was so hungry and sleeping on the road junction. A man called **Othmar** from Switzerland passed by me and asked for my name and whether I had eaten or not. I told him that I was totally hungry. This great man with a lovely heart had established a center, where he could look after street kids. I was taken there. I went with him and requested me to first thereafter; he gave me clothes and even a book to read. He stared at me and said **"you have greatness within you, you will impact others."**

After receiving this good news, my hope was renewed. Even I could become someone important! Tears had to flow out of my eyes and this made me to remember that I had set an ambition of becoming a doctor. At the moment, too much tears had to flow continuously. I re-started school from P.5 and to me, this was like a nightmare. I was a hard working boy because I was eager to achieve my dreams. I spent sleepless nights; to the extent that even my fellow students would complain that I read beyond the required. The boxes turned to mattresses.

I want to tell you that the problem is not related to your origin, what you don't have; what happened to you, the problem is what you are doing now. Everything will come to an end. Never lose hope, God knows you! His favor is on your life. What were boxes turned to mattress and even an airplane. I therefore appeal to you that, the problem is not your origin or what you lack. Everything lies on what you're doing now. Trust only God. Focus only on your future and what you can do at the present to brighten it. By getting help from different people. I continued my studies and completed secondary school. I then went to university.

"Problems are not stop signs, they are guidelines."

- ROBERT H. SCHULLER

"Expect problems and eat them for breakfast."

- ALFRED A. MONTAPERT

"Challenges are what make life interesting and overcoming them is what makes life meaningful."

- JOSHUA J. MARINE

Advice

1. Have hope that even though you're facing challenges, there is happiness. In the future, the problems you're facing will end and the sun will shine.
2. Be aware that God who created you is the One to face the problem. It may be and you will end up victorious.
3. Be courageous of what ever happened to you. You can change anything that happened to you.
4. Be aware that your life is precious and that there is no one who can change, except you.
5. Do not waste your time on what ended. Instead, get what to do now
6. Find friends to be with you during problems or suffering.
7. Learn to think positively and read books that can help you build your hope, watch films that can maintain your life positively.
8. What happens to you can happen to others, more to that; problems are common among us. Take them as opportunities.
9. Don't be overtaken by stress but find what you can do and profit you and even your country. Therefore be firm.

Which Goals Do You Have in Your Life?

If I can be able to achieve my dreams, then how far do you think can you reach? God bless all those servants, who enabled me to achieve goals and dreams. A vote of thanks goes to Ange Condo who brought me with parental love and gave me a picture for my future. You told me that God made me with greatness, "there is something great in me." These words made me have much interest for searching and searching until I got it. Your words was a healing balm to my fear, I could sleep comfortably upon reflecting my future life.

5. Three Lessons I have Learnt in My Life

1. Most of the times, you find when we have dreams of where we want to reach and when we tell people who we trust, that they can give us advice of which people to include our best friends, our relatives, parents, siblings, teachers and friends, they just end up laughing at us, saying that those things are impossible. That we are going to waste our time, that even in our families no one has ever reached anywhere. In so saying, they mean that we are doing nothing. I want to tell you that you should trust no one in your life except yourself. Never have time for anyone who wants to take you backwards or to hide and goals in life *"You must have goals dreams in life and you must to believe in yourself."* I learnt this in the hard way.
2. The second one, as I said in my story, when we reached home and found when a tree has fallen on the house. In order to remove it, we first cut it into many pieces and we pushed one by one till we removed all of the pieces. Now, for the dreams you have or your goals. You are requested to get a piece of paper and a pen. Then you write and thereafter, separate them into parts. You must know which goal you should finish in a day, one month, 3 months, one year and even five years and upwards. On removing the tree, we found a stone that had penetrated the ground. This demanded us to

dig deep, so that we could reach it. Your dreams will demand you to dig deep, so as to achieve them. Nothing is easy. This will require you to use all you have, all energy and resources and when you fail, you must try to make a research of handling it. Never ever give up. Use all you have, do what is required to get what you want in life. *Never give up!*

3. When you have set a goal in your life, it is always not easy to realize it. It requires time and patience with the situation, hard work and being firm. That's the only way to your success. To me, it took more than 18 years in order to achieve my dream (set goal).People told me that you will never achieve anything myself. Some teachers would make me kneel down for 3 hours. I have failed in my studies. My fellow students had nick named me, "A mediocre," because I was not smart. Some students even called me stupid. A doctor who had treated my ear, told my mum one day that I was good for nothing. I grew up having that belief, as true about me. But one day, I decide to do something different my point is that maybe even you will meet many challenges and troubles in your life like mine and many will tell you that, what you are doing is meaningless. That's where you find people becoming weak immediately. They give up their dreams and set goals. What I can tell you here is never and never be disappointed in your life, because of what you meet and even what is happening on you. *The main issue here is to have dreams.* When you happen to meet problems or temptations where one emerges following the other. Don't take a decision of taking alcohol as some do, and they deteriorate their lives, thinking that they are reducing problems.

No, stand firm by the problems you are passing through, They are not hereditary. They are not chronic. Time will come and the sun will shine. Look for the solutions to the problems you are facing. I have known that the problems are common to us all. Everyone has got times, no one has less or more. It's up-to one self and how one reacts. You can never live life, free from problems or troubles. However much you may think that you are escaping, they will still follow you. Or you can meet ahead those, which are worse than the first. You jump one here and find two waiting for you.

I want to address those ones who are baffled with that problem, take a firm stands.

If you stand firm, you will be firm but if troubles disturb you and you accept them, you will be defeated or you yourself will have other destinations. Sometimes you find people who have given themselves to alcohol and others commit suicide, but that's not the right way to deal with problems. Just settle down, get the problem, identify the problem, look all the alternative solutions, collect all information you need, seek help from others and note them on a pieces of paper that you divided into various parts, talk to each problem that you are aware of it and you are there for it. Let it know that you are fighting with it, because you are of great value than a crowd of problems. Take it to be minor or rare, know how it came and how it can be solved. With all that advice put in consideration, success will be yours. It's now your turn to try your level best.

Part 2

10 Habits of Masters of Self-Awareness

It is Your Life and You are the Pilot, Do Something about Your Life

My friend, Mark is married with a child of around five years. Mark worked as a broker. He would wake up early in the morning and come back in the evening and find his baby girl already asleep. Before the child could go to sleep, she would always ask her mum, where the father was because she could rarely see him. Once, Mark was diagnosed with heart disease. The doctors advised him to reduce the work burden he was having and to stop smoking and drinking alcohol, even though he loved them most. They also stopped him from driving, because he could drive under the influence of alcohol and likely to cause accidents and be in conflict with policemen. Thus Mark valued what the doctors said. He started coming home early and gets enough time to play and interact with his daughter.

Once, a friend of me had a party. He invited Mark too. We were great friends from the campus. When the ceremony was due, I was requested to come and assist in the program. But I never knew Mark even though I was going to work with him. They gave me his telephone number and I called him that we are going to be together at the ceremony. There was only two days left for the party. When the day of the party was at hand, we set off for it and did our work well. But in the evening, when we are almost planning to leave, Mark forgot that he was forbidden to take alcohol and he resorted to drinking even more until he was completely drunk and started staggering.

As there were many people, they got hold of him and advised him to be quiet and he listened. He took his car and drove it away. On his way back, it so happened that he had an accident. He was crushed by a big lorry from behind and the car toppled on the side road. The lorry immediately vanished without even taking notice of the accident. As luck would have it, Mark was alone in his car. His wife and child had left the party earlier. In the twinkling of an eye, the police arrived at the scene. They pulled the car from the road side and checked upon the driver; they found him in a serious condition and decided to take him to the hospital. Reaching there, the doctors found his phone in his pocket got the recently dialed numbers. Among the numbers, there was mine. They called me and I quickly rushed to the hospital. On seeing him, he was in a critical condition, almost in a coma. I immediately called his wife. When she saw him, she failed to control herself and started crying bitterly. The doctors tried to comfort her that he was in going to recuperate quickly but all was in vain. We spent the whole night in the hospital and till morning. The wife then went back home to see the child whom she had left alone at home. The child started asking her where the dad was, and she frankly told her that he was admitted to the hospital. On coming back, she took the child with her to see the father.

When the child saw her father, she almost screamed to the extent that the doctors came and requested her to take the child out and she was taken back home. Mark spent almost four days in coma. His child had also failed to eat. On the fifth day, the mother tried to bring the child again, but she was not allowed to take the child inside because of the noise. The mum stood outside on the window where the husband was. The child, on seeing the father on the bed, kept weeping loudly calling, "Dad, dad, wake up and we will play. Dad, I want to play with you. Dad wake up we go home!" When the noise became intense, the father opened his eyes and on peeping through the window, he found that it was his child crying, calling him to come and go home to play with her as was the custom. Mark was deeply agitated; bed ridden as he was and he became speechless for a moment. As it was hard to make any movement of the body, he only nodded his head. He stared at his child and started shedding tears too. When the doctors asked him what had gone wrong, he told them that nothing was wrong. What was painful, after 30 minutes, Mark breathed his last. The doctors informed us of his death and we took the corpse home.

When it was time for the burial, his wife brought the medical report that confirmed a heart attack. Among the guidelines to follow, there was, "there is nobody who can take charge of your life. It's yours. Learn how to handle and care for your life. Do physical exercises daily and eat well. Give your life direction and basic principles for good health." When the funeral was over, I sat down carefully and did a flash back. I found out that thousands of people are jokingly playing with their lives. They take it any how they want as if it doesn't belong to them. But believe it or not, your life remains your life and you are the pilot. If you handle it carelessly, you will suffer the consequence. You cannot escape. Many drive under the influence of alcohol, or abuse drugs on the top, knowing its side effects. But when sickness comes, they start regretting. Still others don't want to do anything; they want to remain in their poverty state. They don't want to study, they are lazy but the end result of all those, in finishing all your life without achieving anything. I do believe that God has got beautiful plans for us, but it depends on how we use our efforts. Choose what to do and give your life direction. Have a purpose in life. Have a mission and vision for your future.

Advice

- Life is a talent God bestowed you, which has a time limit.
- Life will be valuable not only to you but to others, as far as you have a vision and set goals.
- As it is impossible to drive a car without petrol, we should not live without aims or dreams.
- In giving your life direction, intangible things will change to tangible ones.

Meaning of Life

You have been given life to live it fully and discover your calling. Life is a platform of becoming a better person, every single day. Life presents you daily gifts to grow and prosper. The word life itself has a deep meaning in it. **L** stands for look, **I** stands for inside, **F** means for and **E** stands for enlightenment. Life means looking inside for enlightenment. Living a happy and abundant life is your birthright. Life is an awesome opportunity, to learn new possibilities about helping others. Life is like a platform that is given to you. Life gives you everything when you start looking within your own self. One gets nothing except worldly illusions, when he looks outside, while one gets everything within his own self when he looks within his own self. You have all the answers within yourself. No one from the outside can make you happy and prosperous, until you do not connect to your inner self. Without a rich inner life, expecting a rich outer life is pure foolishness.

You can respect life by becoming a passionate student of self-awareness. For your growth and happiness, 10 habits of masters of self-awareness are presented. Self-awareness means becoming aware about your real self. You are originally powerful and unique in this whole world. Once you commit yourself to understand this eternal truth of your inner power and uniqueness, you start feeling peace, love, happiness and abundance within you.

Discover Your Calling

As per a famous saying, there are two wonderful days in the life of a person. The first one is when he gets birth in this beautiful world and the second one is when he finds his calling. Your calling means your way of shining in this world. Your calling means your passion. Your calling means your style of serving humanity. Your calling means your way of adding values in the lives of people. Calling is something which is essential to discover, to prosper in life. You can easily discover your calling by consistently becoming a sincere student of your own self-development, in a few years. There are books, blogs and interviews available to help you in knowing your calling. We have respectfully shared a list of books and names of enlightened people who will definitely help you in finding your real reason to succeed in life. Make it clear, without discovering your calling you will struggle in life. But on the other hand, once you discover your calling, you start relishing the knowledge that life is given to you for a special reason.

Serve Humanity

Service is the synonym of success. Serve to succeed. Serve to soar. Serve to prosper. Serve to live an abundant life. Serve to discover your calling. Serve to add fortune in your life. Find ways helping others. Think about adding values in the lives of people. Those who serve always succeed. They create their own luck. We respectfully advise you to please understand the whole philosophy of wealth. Without clearly understanding the concept of wealth, it is simply impossible to achieve massive wealth. There is a simple yet powerful principle behind creating massive wealth in your life which is; your outer wealth is a clear reflection of your inner wealth. Finding inner wealth is a process that takes years to happen. Finding inner wealth is all about making yourself able to achieve wealth in life. Finding inner wealth is all about realizing your inner infinite resources. Finding inner wealth is about realizing your true purpose of taking birth in this world. Understand your importance in this world. You are not here to struggle. You are not here to live an empty life. You are not here to curse yourself. You are not here to think like life is a test. There is a process of making yourself able to get the results that you naturally deserve to get in life

10. Powerful Lessons about Money Making

1. Money making is an art, not a luck factor.
2. Like other subjects, it can also be learnt.
3. Money making is directly related to your financial awareness.

4. You have to learn more about your work to earn more.
5. Principles of money making are universally same.
6. If you do what your heart says then money making is extremely easy.
7. If you are a great network builder again money making is very easy.
8. Most important, your thoughts about money.
9. Remember, what Napoleon Hill said in his great book, "Think and Grow Rich," you have to attract money, because money has no power of its own.
10. For making money, being only interested in making money doesn't work for you, for making money you have to be dedicated towards it.

10 Habits of Masters of Self-Awareness

1. Masters of self-awareness are clear about what they want out of life.
2. Are passionate dreamers.
3. Are perfect networkers.
4. Do friendship with people who are also masters of self-awareness.
5. Always look for new ideas and ready to do self-development continuously.
6. Love and respect other people and help them in growing in life.
7. Use every inner resource that they have got in life.
8. Believes in abundance and work with never ending spirit.
9. Are awesome speakers and presenters of ideas.
10. Masters of self-awareness love feedback.

Habit 1: Masters of Self-Awareness are Clear about What They Want Out of Life

Clarity precedes mastery. Clarity comes first to you, then mastery visits you. The habit of clarity is the habit of mastery. People with self-awareness as their core focus, achieve far more than an ordinary person can expect to achieve in life. Mahatma Gandhi is a great example of this habit. This great visionary was clear about what he wanted out of his life. He was exceptionally clear about his vision. He achieved his vision at the end. To achieve, one must have a clear mind about what to achieve.

Practice this master habit today by clearing your mind about your goals in life. Clear what you want out of life. Without a clear direction and goal, one is destined to fail in life.

Remember, success is not away from you, but you are away from success. You have to attract your desired results first by becoming clear about them. Hardly 5% people are there in this world, which is clear about what they are searching in their lives and they are exactly getting the same.

Masters of self-awareness practice this iron principle of clarity, every day in their lives. Take a. How do you want to live your life? What do you want to become in the next five years? Clarity gives you confidence. Clarity of goals presents you a gift of infinite inner power. If you are serious about achieving grand goals in life, then you must be clear about your primary goals in life.

With clear goals, you get clear focus. With clear focus, you win half of the game in the beginning itself. With clarity of your life goals, you become unstoppable. Extraordinary people are only ordinary people with a laser like focus on their life goals. One can achieve a worthy goal in life if he is crystal clear about achieving it.

Habit 2: Masters of Self-Awareness are Exceptional Networkers

Your network speaks about your net worth. Network gives you growth and new opportunities to expand yourself. You must be ready to add new people in your life, at all stages. New people bring new possibilities in your life. Your network is the true measure of your relation making ability. Business is all about relationships. Success is all about relation making. You must focus on expanding your network.

Your network means the group of people you earn in life. More you grow your network, more you network gives you growth. Masters of self-awareness are much concerned about adding new and visionary people in their lives at all stages.

Your network decides your happiness level, fulfillment level, wealth and contribution. You learn to respect life by people of your network.

You must be a good networker. You must be a god communicator. You must be able to respect other people feelings. You must be willing to create a network of self-awareness based people. You must be willing to live an epic life. You must be willing to attract people who can surely help in turning your dreams into reality. Every champion focuses more on relationship building with other champions. Every peak performer focuses on attracting other peak performers in his life.

Habit 3: Masters of Self-Awareness Learn Every Single Day

Learners are earners. Leaners become leaders. Learn to lead. Learn to grow. Learn to expand. Learn to evolve. Learn to feel blessed in life. Learning is all about knowing your own ignorance. Learning is leading. Learning is growing. Learn every single day. Learn like crazy. Become a serious student of self-development. Commit to know yourself every single day. Dedicate yourself towards knowing your inner self. Learn about your inner possibilities. Learn about your inner powers. Learn about your inner infinite creative potential. Learn about your blessings. Learn about your strengths. Learn about what you can achieve in life.

Learners live longer. Learners discover. Learners innovate. Learners become visionaries. Learn about public speaking. Learn about your own inner development.

Read books on self-help. Read books on success. Read books on leadership. Read books on how to discover you calling. Read books on how to be a meaningful person. Read books on inner peace. Read books on how to find inner power. Read books on gratitude. Read books on creative thinking. Read books on productive habits. Read books on meditation.

Stay learning till your last breathe. Be a lifelong learner. Read something inspirational to stay positive every single day. Learn to stay motivated. Learn about your own inner possibilities to grow exponentially in life. Learn how to convert your setbacks into stepping stones. Learn how to see adversities as new possibilities to grow. Learn how to be an enlightened being. Learn to learn from your mistakes. Learn how you can take profit from your mistakes. Learn to speak to make others realize their respect and honor.

Habit 4: Masters of Self-Awareness are Passionate Dreamers

Dream to achieve. Dream of living a better life. Dream of becoming a better person every single day. Make your dream book. Write your dreams. Dream more dreams. Be a passionate dreamer. Dreamers win. Dreamers create. Dreams give you energy. Dreams gifts you strength. Dreams give ability to grow in life.

People with dreams are unstoppable. Live your dreams. Dream of giving your best to mankind. Dream of giving respect to everyone. Dream of staying grateful in life. Dream of living a full life. Dream of living an epic life. Dream of serving humanity. Dream of creating your destiny. Dream of discovering your calling. Dream of living a totally awakened life. Dream of becoming an enlightened being. Dream of discovering your inner beauty. Dream of giving unconditional love to everyone you meet. Dream of looking for opportunities in your difficulties. Be a creative dreamer. Get at least one dream every day. Respect your dreams. Dream first, to achieve later. Men of achievement are men of dreams. Your dreams give your inner light. Your dreams give you motivation. Invest in dreaming. Adopt the habit of creative dreaming. Take time to dream. Be a dreamer of epic life.

Habit 5: Masters of Self-Awareness are Strong Believers of Abundance

One eye opening fact about life is it has enough for every single person. Life is full of infinite opportunities. Life is full of infinite possibilities. Life has enough for you. There is no lack in this world. World is full of great treasures. You have been taught to think in limits by your surroundings. Your first job is to unchain your thoughts. Hard work is essential to succeed but abundance mindset is also a must in life. Life wants you to grow. Life wants you to live a happy life. Life wants you to live an epic life. Life wants you to stay fit and active every single day. There is infinite wealth available to every single one. Believe in abundance. Believe that life is full of infinite opportunities. Use words like infinite, unlimited, wide, huge, massive and broad. If you believe that resources of this world are limited then we request you to please think over it again. Be an optimist about life. Be hopeful about life. Be hopeful about yours own self. There is an iron law of abundance that says, there are no limits to which you can improve hence there are no limits to that you can achieve in life. You deserve to have abundance in life.

Know life. Know yourself. Know the infiniteness of life. Know your limitlessness. Your true nature is limitless. You have infinite greatness within you. You have abundance within you. You are limited that is your false belief. You can achieve only in limits in life that is your false belief. Your share of happiness, wealth and health is infinite. Your energy to perform things is infinite. Your ability to grow every single day is infinite. Your potential to elevate your lifestyle is infinite. Your inner awesomeness is infinite. Your capacity to serve mankind is infinite. Your ability to prosper your life is infinite. Your ability to learn new things in life is infinite. Your ability to stay grateful towards life is infinite. Your ability to love others is infinite. Your power to turn your dreams into reality is infinite. Your ability to enlighten your life is infinite.

Habit 6: Masters of Self-Awareness Love People Unconditionally

If someone behaves well to you, behave well in return. If someone behaves badly to you, still behave well in return. Masters of self-awareness do this. What you do is your karma. What others do is their karma. Spread love everywhere. Be a life time brand ambassador of love, peace, abundance, politeness, patience, respect and honor. Give love to everyone. Give respect to everyone. To lead people love them. To inspire people love them. To make people aware about your true self-love them. Love is everything. Being able to love people is real richness.

Life is all about treating people with love and honor. Love people. Care people. Honor people. Respect people. Every single person on this earth is connected to you. Every single person is interconnected. Make love your biggest tool to win. Make love to your asset. Make love your ultimate possession. Become a lover of mankind. Become a true appreciator of people. Appreciate people naturally. Create a culture of loving others everywhere. Loving others is living wisdom. Dedicate yourself to love others.

If you really want to help people, love them. Love yourself. Respect yourself. Discover yourself. Explore yourself. Love your parents. Love your friends. Love your dreams. Love your life. Instead of judging people, love them. Instead of comparing people, love them. Lovers live longer. Be a lover of truth. Be a lover of inner peace. Be a lover of inner freedom. Be a lover of inner wisdom. Be a lover of abundance. Be a lover of self-development. Be a lover of service to society. Be a lover of enlightenment. Be a lover of inner awakening. Be a lover of unconditional respect giving. Be a lover of lifelong learning. Be a lover of dreaming. Be a lover of self-awareness.

Habit 7: Masters of Self-Awareness Respect Their Four Ultimate Blessings of Life

Life blesses you with four ultimate gifts every single day. These four gifts are your heart, mind, body and soul. The one who respects and cares these four gifts on daily basis is a true master of self-awareness. To open yourself towards the ways of respecting these gifts, we are sharing the ways with you. Sharing these eternal success principles with you is our calling. We took birth to help you in knowing your inner reality. We are highly excited to let you know that you are a masterpiece.

To respect your heart every day, give respect to everyone you meet daily. When you give respect, care and honor to others, your heart gets respect and ultimate care in return. To make your heart young forever, give respect to people forever. Staying young forever is totally in your control. Becoming a person of absolute luck is in your reach. When you give respect to others, you become lucky. When you care others, you make yourself most alive. When you give happiness to others, you get ultimate happiness in return.

To give respect to your mind, give it knowledge every day. Be a lifelong learner to care your mind. Your mind needs constant learning to stay younger. Once you start learning eternal success principles, you start getting ultimate fulfillment in life. Your mind is your biggest and ultimate possession. Give your mind an active and creative diet of pure thoughts every day. Make your mind your servant. Do not let your mind to become your master.

To respect your body, stay fit. Exercise every day to appreciate your body. Eat natural and active food to stay active. Having a healthy body is like having abundance in life. Your body is naturally made to stay fit, active and healthy. It is your own ignorance of this precious blessing when you feel ill, inactive and weak. Become rich in taking care of your body. Become aware about importance of staying active and healthy in life. You feel confident, when you are active.

To respect your soul, do something good to others every day. Selfishness stops you to feed your soul. Selflessness is the ultimate food for your soul. When you serve others, you grow exponentially. When you help others, you create your luck. When you help others, you actually help your own self. Your serving ability decides your height of achievements. Your serving ability is your growing ability. When you serve, you soar. When you elevate others, you become truly unstoppable.

Heart, mind, body and soul are ultimate blessings that you get in life. By dedicating yourself to respect all these four blessings every single day, you for sure become a master of self-awareness.

Habit 8: Masters of Self-Awareness Are Capable of Expressing Themselves to the World

Only when you express your true talent, you get rewards in return. If you are unable to express your talents, then it will be understood that you do not have any talent. Becoming a good presenter is very essential. You must discover your calling. You must find your passion. Actually, your passion is your gift to this world. Your calling is your ultimate blessing to the whole world. You are not on this earth to struggle, to fight with poverty or to cry on your fate. You are here to discover your calling. Until you do not express your heart, you will remain unfulfilled. You want expression of your true inner self. Whenever you find opportunities to express yourself you feel satisfied.

True aim of getting life is becoming able to give back to mankind. Nature has blessed you with unique talents and inner infinite possibilities. Your job is to open your inner talents. You job is to explore your inner life. Once you learn the art of expressing your inner self you will shine on every platform. Lady Gaga, Bill Gates, William Shakespeare, Sachin Tendulkar and Oprah Winfrey, all masters of self-awareness, are highly successful and fulfilled because they have ways of expressing their inner infinite creative potential. You have that potential unrecognized and dormant. You have to learn the ways of sharing it with the world. Focus on art of expressing your true talents. If you believe that you got birth to do something extraordinary believe us you will certainly do that. Your belief creates your true reality. You create your destiny. You create your fate. You choose your lifestyle. Become aware about your inner gifts. Have desire in you to serve mankind with the help of your inner gifts.

Habit 9: Masters of Self-Awareness Surround Themselves with People Who Love Truth

Your friends play a vital role in your life. There is a famous saying that says, "After five years, your level of success will be revealed by your friends and books you experience within that duration," The point is very clear that you get influenced by each and every friend of yours. People who are very conscious about their happiness and success always love to be with people who love truth.

To become truly successful, you must know the truth. Your friends can play a crucial role in helping you in knowing the truth. The truth of life is that you are powerful. You have greatness within you. You are totally capable of turning your dreams into reality. You are totally able to live a life of your dreams. Your parents, friends and childhood conditioning teach you something else. They drill into you that you are not able. You are not talented. You have something wrong in you. You cannot become a celebrity. You do not deserve to live an epic life.

Make friends who respect themselves. Make friends who love themselves. Make friends who are very much clear about their role in life. Believe us; your friends are highly important in your life. Make friends who help you in growing your awareness every single day. Make friends who motivate you to go further and further in life. Make friends who help you in realizing your inner self. Make friends who inspire you to go deep in your own self. Make friends who love you unconditionally.

Make truth your best friend. Make your own inner self your best friend. Make self-help books your best friends. Make self-development rituals your best friends. No one in this whole world is responsible for your success or failure. You have to take responsibility of your life in your hands. Become your own best friend. Learn appreciating your true inner talents. You have a treasure inside you. Your friends can really help you in reaching this treasure. The moment you get realization about your inner life, you start saying, "thank you," to the whole universe.

Choose friends wisely, because they help you in choosing your destiny. Choose wise friends to live life wisely. Choose friends who always give you confidence, energy and creative ideas.

Habit 10: Masters of Self-Awareness Take Regular Feedback of Their Own Selves

Become your own master. Become your own teacher. Become your own mentor. Become a leader of your life.

Become a designer of your life. Adopt habit of taking your regular feedback. Record your daily progress. Record your daily learning on paper. Write your daily learning.

To live an epic life, you must take regular feedback of your own daily life. You cannot ignore not taking your daily feedback. Once you start writing or recording your own daily insights, you start making your life a grand one. Life is given to you and now it is up-to you how you take it. Adopt a habit of taking pictures of your daily growth activities. Adopt the habit of writing your daily progress journal.

Make your annual learning plans. Every day you get infinite opportunities to grow more in life but because you do not have the habit of recording those opportunities you tend to miss them daily. Do not pass your life. Do not expect luck to give you a grand life. Do not expect miracle to happen from outside you. Do not expect a grand life accidently. You have to make those changes happen by your own efforts. You have to take the lead role in your life. You have to become aware about your own inner possibilities. You have to record your daily learning to get wise life lessons out of them. You have to become a daily student of your own success. You have to take yourself on the road to success.

Commit to make your life a grand one. Commit to live a fulfilled life. Commit to live a life of purpose. Commit to live a life of values. Commit to live a life of abundance. Commit to discover your inner treasures. Commit to serve humanity. Commit to stay thankful to life.

To become a master of self-awareness, start taking daily feedback of your own learning. Believe us, you are a special and unique masterpiece.

Part 3

Self-Awareness

1. There is Potential within You

"Everyone has inside of him a piece of good news. The good news is that you don't know how great you can be! How much you can love! What you can accomplish! And what your potential is!"

- ANNE FRANK

We are all gifted with different and various capabilities that can lead us to make a difference and impact our personal life and society, as well. As Marie Curie said, "we must believe that we are gifted for something and that this thing at whatever cost, must be attained." This is the reason why we see around us people who succeed in whatever they do without any real base, for example, studies, capital or any other support. We use to say that disability is not inability referring to persons with disabilities, forgetting that even us who look physically fit have the kind of disability of not believing in ourselves.

- The potential in you is something special that you are created with, something that differentiates you from other people around you and much more something that only you is able to unlock.
- Your potential is all you can be but you have not become yet, all you could do but you have not done yet. And remember that for every head that stands, there is potential and greatness within.

Failing to identify the potential in us make us less confident about ourselves. In such conditions, we tend to see, think or say that others are better than us. This is bad because we see ourselves as losers by birth. When I was in secondary school, I used to be a good runner, I could easily get the first or second place at the school level and I saw that as nothing, because all I could get from the race was a good grade in sports and applauses from the audience. One day, I was selected to represent my school in a running race at the national level. The idea of running together with famous runners from famous schools gave me a terrible panic, that I refused the offer. I suggested that instead, they could take the person who was second to me, with the reason that I was very small, and I was not used to big races among other pretexts. Then I was called to the headmaster's office, to explain my attitude. I expected the headmaster to get mad at me and order me to attend the race or get suspended. Instead, he asked me to have a seat and started to lecture me. "Ben, I know you're a good runner and I believe you can represent us well, all you have to do is to believe in yourself too. Each and every person in this school believes in you, but you are failing to believe in that little traits that makes you different from all those students that you leave behind when you are running." Then he gave me some time to think about it and come back to tell him of my decision.

I could not figure out what the headmaster meant by the little traits that differentiates me from the rest of students, especially those of whom I leave behind when running. I wanted to accept it but when I remembered the names of students that I have heard about from famous schools, I hesitated. I could see myself in imagination taking the last place and bringing shame on my school. I could imagine how much people who believed in me as the headmaster said, will get disappointed within just a few seconds of the one hundred meter race. *"Let it be someone else,"* I said in my heart. The headmaster called me again and at his encouraging words, I decided to run. Together with other sportsmen, we started our final preparations and I was sure I was doing well. Then the due date arrived.

We had to travel from Gitarama to Kigali and we were supposed to spend in the city, the whole weekend which was exciting for all of us. But I was in deep thoughts. When the day arrived, we went to take our running numbers. I was given number 19. I was in a group of fourteen people who were in 100m race. I could not believe myself between more well-known runners and I was somehow excited and afraid, at the same time. I was assuming that no one is afraid of me, but I was afraid of them. When we went in the field, and when I looked in the stadium seats, I saw a few students from my school, encouraging me. I looked up and remembered the headmaster's lecture and I said to myself, that I had to keep the trust that all those people put in me. I was determined to do my best and I started to realize that other runners were also somehow nervous and anxious. I then realized that I knew what they were capable of, but they were not aware about my capabilities and I took advantage of that. After few minutes, I was declared the second of the race. From this story, I need you to understand the importance of the word,

"Potential." This means that since I was little, I had the capacity of developing into a good runner, and that is the potential in me. However, I had not realized that potential in me, until I realized that I could beat even famous runners.

After I was able to identify the potential in me, I worked hard on it, so that I get to be identified as a good runner. Is it possible that other people identify the potential in you before you even notice it? The answer is, yes. Sometimes we hear people talking about fields that we are good at, or activities that we accomplish successfully, or even when we are working in groups, you find out that your team members are not confident to accomplish something without your support or presence. All that is because they believe you've the capacities in you. Such perceptions can help one to unlock the potential in him or her, only if the person pays attention to it and find out why some people consider him or her capable of doing or performing an activity successfully. Have you ever asked yourself why your team members, colleagues, siblings or workmates consider you in the way they do? Had they many times considered you as good in the same field? If the answer is yes, then you should be in the right path to unlock the potential in you. To unlock the potential means to be aware of all capacities in you and work hard on them, to shape a carrier that will define you in the future.

Some people always tend to say that their future is dark, that life is hard and many others, disappointing. Such people are in danger of sticking their lives on the wall of poverty and it will be hard to remove them. As I said before, such people consider themselves losers by birth and think that nothing can change their situation, except when someone else like the government, or family members come with something to nourish them. That is not good, let us remember that our lives only belong to ourselves and we are our PILOT. No one is responsible for our misery, but ourselves. **In that case I would suggest the following:**

- Take a hundred percent responsibility for your life by making positive decisions.
- Start to look inside yourself and around you to identify the potential in you.
- Give up all kind of excuses that prevent you to work hard.
- Stop blaming people or any situation to cause your misery.
- Remember that if you keep on doing thing in the same ways you do them, you will keep on getting the some results.
- Don't terminate what you once started.
- Have principles governing your life.
- Program yourself in the work you do.
- Practice what you love rather than doing what others did.
- Set simple goals towards your dreams.

Three Ways to Push Yourself for a Big Achievement

i. Be more focused on yourself

There is something I've realized among people, which is quite surprising. How a person spends all his entire time in things like jobs, studies, business and many other activities, but fail to get the time for them, searching for every knowledge, here and there, revising all literature possible in their profession, attending seminars and workshops about leadership and communication skills. Due to the fact that this global world we are living in requires such skills. When you make it a habit, in three or five years you will find yourself being an expert in your field and win more people. The achievement can be great, as a result of focusing on yourself. Be more focus on yourself.

ii. Develop the courage to push yourself to the next level

In most circumstances, one finds it hard to perform some activities, due to the fear of the outcomes which may either be good or bad. And yet the things we fear are the things which we ought to do. This requires us to develop a spirit of courage to push ourselves to do the most essential things in our lives. Failure to do so does not work, as there is no one else to do it for us. If we want to achieve something in life, we need to change our attitudes and work on our plans, ourselves. I am sure if we develop this courage, we shall achieve what we want.

iii. Develop the courage to seek help from others

People normally say that, "asking leads to understanding." It is through asking that we gain understanding of things, we are ignorant of. When you don't ask, you gain nothing. Seeking information you don't know, doesn't mean you're a fool, it's not. Instead, you will be learning if you want to progress in your studies, life, or any kind of business. It's advisable to seek for assistance from those, who are more experienced in that field. If you obey this, you will be placing yourself on the side of the great achievers, worldwide.

2. Say Yes for Your Life

You must be flexible with your life, your dreams and your mistakes and reform them to your business from today. Don't bring the issue of saying that there is no capital. What matters is only the way forward. Say yes to your Diploma,

Degree, Masters and PhD, yes to success, yes to revision and retrieve what you have revised. Don't reflect much on the evils of the past. Redeem the present. Be focused to make a difference to your our life. Don't under estimate yourself that you can do nothing. **Your life is a book full of indefinite pages, many of which** are **still closed**. There remains another chance for you to achieve something, so make a decision today.

Here are Some of the Questions You need to First Ask Yourself.

1. How do you wish your life to be? (Make a move of your life, past, present and future). Are you satisfied with your life with where you are (professional, financial, physical, social etc.)?
2. After analyzing the film of your life, which thing do you feel you can do or change towards your success and happy life?
3. Write them down on pieces of paper and write the steps you can take against each, right now.
4. Do research; seek advice from those with more experience.
5. Take a big step to make things happen. Don't live an indolent life, waiting for others to occupy your responsibilities. You are solely the key holder of all your affairs. Someone said that, "if you do something, something will happen, but if you don't do anything, nothing will happen." Another said that, God helps those who help themselves."
6. Keep yourself in a positive manner. I have found that the challenges we pass through, things we watch on television, things we hear on the radio and even news

we come across from others, are either constructive or destructive. To a large extent, many are stricken with the challenges of the past and you find those people giving them a room, as part of their being. My advice concerning this situation that has hindered a majority of us from success is to leave the past alone. Forget the evil of the past and look forward. What has passed has passed. Let all that not disturb you, forget all about your mistakes and start a new life. Don't let your mind be overcome by corrupt thoughts. If these thoughts recur, try some sport, watch intellectual films, mingle with your friends, or sing your favorite songs.

3. How to Discover Your Talents

We have talked much about the potential in you which also relates to the talent in you, because the potential is reflected through the talent. In this chapter I will not try to convince you that you have one or more talents. Instead, I will show you how to discover your talents and use those to achieve much more, as it is said that, "you have to be willing to do the things you have never done before, in other to get the things you never had before." We are going to be guided by the story in the Bible, found in Matthew 25:14–30. The story makes a good example of the importance of using our talents for gain.

The story talks about a king who planned to travel to a far country. Then, he called his servants and offered them his belongings. He gave to the first, five talents, the second two and the third, one. He distributed the talents according to their abilities and strengths, and then he left. This is the same way, God when creating us, gave us talents that will help us to achieve whatever we will dream of, in our life according to our strength and potential.

The king could have chosen to go with his belongings, but yet he distributed them. This means that there is something that he wanted from his servants but did not tell them. Each and every one had the task of finding what the king wanted. The same thing happens to us. We sit there and wait for either our parents, or someone else to tell us what to do. As I said before, many people do things because someone else is doing so, or simply because it is the only activity that presented itself, when the talent that we have been given is still sleeping in ourselves.

This is mainly caused by the fact that many of us do not know how to identify our talents. Talent is something that you are passionate about, something that you love to do and feel good when you do it. These tips will help you to identify your talents:

i. Find something in your life that you find easy to do, and that you do more frequently.

People are different in performing different tasks or activities. There must be an activity that you find easy to do when others perceive it as difficult. Take a note of that and start to work hard on it. That's where your talent is hidden. For example, whenever you take a pen and a paper you find yourself drawing patterns that finally make sense to someone, or you find yourself exploring a drawing that you desire to copy. Then drawing is your talent. All you have to do is to work hard on your drawing skills and there you go. You start to design or sell your drawings.

ii. Ask your friends

This is very important when you are not able to identify your talents. Friends or family members, who are with you most of the time, can help. Ask them to tell you about things they consider you are talented in or good at. Do not make mistakes by asking friends who always criticize you, gossip about you, who only worry about their life and who complain so much. These people can misguide you. You must ask those, who have always been at your side and who encouraged you in one or more activities. Note one by one, what the real friends are going to tell you and compare with what you found for yourself.

iii. Look what other people admire about you all the time

I remember when I was in university in MMU in India. We had one guy that we all relied upon, when it came to electricity problems. Maybe a lamp in your room is not functioning. Then you had to go to him and immediately he fixed the problem. One day, after he helped me, I told him if he had ever considered to learn more about electricity and make it a career. He said "No, I like the electricity field, but that is not my talent." I told him that sometimes we are not able to identify our talents, but our friends do. I advised him to consider the fact that everyone in the campus referred to him as the "electrician guy." It was simply because we admired his talent. The same thing can be applied to you; how many people who come to you asking for some help? How many times have people applauded you for the same activity? Try to listen to what people say about you and your activities and note down whatever you find out. Then compare with those that you found before. I am sure you are going to notice the most common observation and that might be your talent.

iv. Find that something that you enjoy most and feel happy to do

Passion is very important when it comes to talent. You are passionate with an activity when you can do it effortlessly and can spend much of your time on it, regardless of what you can get from it. Take your time to analyze something that you enjoy most, when you are doing it. For me, I like to write. I can spend all the day writing and feel happy about it. Look for that thing that you have passion for and focus on it.

It might be possible that after analyzing all these tips you find that you have more than one talent. Then redo the exercise and find out which one is dominant. After you decide on it, start practicing it, work hard on it and if necessary learn more about it. In order to gain more from the talent, it might possible that it requires you to have academic papers in that field. So you will need to invest in nurturing your talent by going to school to be a professional. Going back to our story, the king came back and wanted the three servants to present what they became of his talents. The first servant was in a good position, because he used the five received talents and presented to the king, five more talents that he got from trading the received talents. The same thing happened to the second who presented two more talents, but the third was ashamed and became harsh and undisciplined before the king. And he said, Then he which had received the one talent came and said, Lord, I knew that thou art an hard man, reaping where thou hast not sown, and gathering where thou hast not strewed" (Matthew 25:24, king James Version).

And he returned to the king the same one talent that he had, until the king's return. The language of this lazy servant looked much like that of people who fail to use their talents and spend their time complaining about those who successfully used their talents and God blessed them from their hard work.

I believe that all us we have greatness of potential within ourselves and we see them through talents. When you discover them and work hard to get them right, the change will happen immediately. You were born with them but you have not used them. This is the time, start practicing, and enjoy gaining and being blessed from something that you like.

4. Self-Evaluation and Self-Image

When I was in secondary school, our headmaster used to ask us about ourselves. All of us knew that answers to his questions were simple. We identified ourselves by our names in full, our parents' names and our current careers. Then the headmaster was not satisfied with our answers and encouraged us to identify ourselves differently by replacing our parents' names by our hobbies and goals. For example, one could say his name, and add that he is a student, whose goal is to become a doctor and who likes to play football and to read books. I did not understand the purpose of the headmaster, before I realized that as I kept on introducing myself as a future doctor, I had the courage to not to disappoint myself, or to let down people who encouraged my dream.

Self-evaluation is a process of going inside ourselves and identifying what we have, the mistakes that we no longer want to commit and what we lack in order, to achieve our goals in life. Self-evaluation is all about answering questions like: Who is the person that I am becoming? Why am I becoming so? What do I need to help me become who I want to be? What are my strengths and weaknesses? Am I in the right path or not? In self-evaluation, do not bother thinking about people around you, just focus on yourself. Some people do not care about anything. They think that as long as they can earn a little, they have to come up with any bad feeling and mistreatment that they face. Such people wake up-to go to the jobs that they don't like, work with people that they don't like, get the salary that they are not happy with and just continue with such a life full of complains. They allow themselves to commit unnecessary sins that they could have been able to avoid, only if they evaluated themselves and found out what was their real value. They believe that life is to go to school, get a degree, get a job, get married, have children, educate them, retire and die. Yes, those steps are also part of life but have you lived happily? Happiness and satisfaction also matters.

You will know you are unhappy with your career when you will find yourself spending your time doing and enjoying something that is completely different from your career. For example, a businessman who can spend the best part of his time drawing dresses for women. Such a person has missed the career of a designer, either because his parents insisted on him studying and doing business, when he really liked to draw, since his childhood. And the problem here was not his parents, but the person himself who let his parents cover his self-evaluation. Self-evaluation helps us to create a self-image that goes together with our dreams and desires. Self-image simply means "what you see in yourself." It refers to how we feel and react about ourselves. It is the mental picture of yourself and the way you see yourself morally and physically in terms of talents, intelligence, beauty, ambitions, competence, confidence, courage, creativity, energy, friendship, happiness, honesty, helpfulness, logic, optimism, patience, reason, resource, trust and responsibility.

Sadly, many of us always see themselves in mirrors of negativity. They don't have a good picture of themselves. They don't like themselves. But my question is, if you don't like yourself, who will? Following are common negative self-image descriptions:

- Am not talented.
- I don't have a good personality.
- I am very bad.
- I am not like others.
- I am small.
- I am fat.
- No good things happen to me.
- I am not attractive.
- I have done many mistakes.
- I am not educated.
- I am not capable.
- I am not... I am not... I am not...the list is long.

All these people do, is to complain about themselves, gossip about others and criticize everything that happens around them. Research has found that the physical looks take ten percent, when internal fitness take ninety percent when it comes to success. This means that the way you see yourself, will contribute ninety percent to your success and how others see you, will contribute ten percent. But the problem here is we like to focus on our external qualities or beauty, rather than spending our time constructing our internal fitness. The truth here is that the level of your internal fitness will be manifested on your physical looks through your confidence.

My advice here is that if you want to succeed in your life, or to achieve any kind of dreams or goals you have, either in business, education or relationship, you have to be confident of who you are, how you look and what you have. You are called to have a positive self-image about yourself and be sure about it. The f**ollowing ten tips are going to help you to construct and improve your positive self-image.**

- Never criticize yourself for mistakes you made in the past: Yes, you did so many mistakes, fine, but remember it was in the past, you are no longer living there. Everyone makes mistakes; you are neither the first nor the last.
- Forgive yourself and promise yourself to change for the good.
- Stop listening to people who influenced you to do your mistakes and those who keep reminding you, of your mistakes.
- Drop those friends who always speak negatively of you. Replace them with those who understand your mistakes and are willing to help you, change for the good. Remember, a true friend is the one who will be there when you need him or her.
- Feel good about yourself: black, white, skinny, fat, or any trait that might make you feel low, you don't have to care. Feel good and satisfied of how you look and you

will live long. You have to love yourself, no matter what, because if you fail, no one will do that for you.

- Strive to get more and more by dreaming big and learn to take decisions that will lead you where you want to go.
- Be honest and realistic about yourself.
- Keep doing the good things everyday: take time every day to focus on positive things and remind yourself to do good to you and to others.
- Never blame others for something bad happening to you. Just remind yourself that misfortunes are part of human life.
- Never criticize others if you cannot help them to correct their mistakes.

Just be You

Ange Umutoni my adoptive mother did a significant work in creating hope and strong believe in me. She used to said that, God endowed me with great gifts and talents which I can use to achieve anything in my life. As my custom was, I used to pass by her home or at her workplace after class to say farewell. I am reminded of one incident, when we were seated in her office. It was afternoon. Weld a conversation and finally she asked me a question, "Ben, it's true you told me that you want to study and become a doctor, or ambassador or a State minister, tell me one thing, What you are doing now. Will that enable you achieve your aim?" The question seemed not to be clear to me and I asked for further elaboration. She again inquired of me to frankly enlighten to her, the way forwards the achievement of my aims.

"See now, I have come to say farewell to you and continue school for studies. When at school, I can't be careless. From the beginning of the semester, I do not want to waste any minute. I want to prepare myself for the exams and among the aims I set for my life. Failing is not there. I will leave no stone unturned in order to be successful in my studies. "How do you revise?" she asked me. "When I am at school, I do profit my time whether in difficulties or in peace, when others go to waste time. I try my level best to utilize that time." She laughed and told me "Never forget who you are." Here, I mean that don't forget where you are heading and above all your vision and dreams.

"At school, I hear that you find amazing things, which make students not to concentrate much on their studies, thereby failing. Not because they are dull, but because they waste their time in unprofitable things. Never follow their example; be in their behavior or in whatever they do, as far as they are useless. Never should I hear that you are misled by other malicious students.

Take note from your teachers, respect them. Don't try disobeying rules and regulations of students, because I want you to be a responsible man and become useful to others and your country, in general. All this will happen through education. Do you remember your story How life was so hard to you after the genocide against Tutsi in our country. Do you remember how you were meandering the entire way, carrying luggage in order to get food to eat, got beaten like a wild dog, called as a thief, slept on boxes as your mattress? And during the rainy season, you used to sleep on the verandahs of shops. Nobody can believe that you can reach where you are! Do not forget that, do hear me?" I said, "Yes I do Mum."

"However, you won't achieve anything when you don't work hard; this calls for transformation because you can't get something for luck, but you can create luck by working hard. Don't stress yourself when you see that some students who are well off, be it in terms of money, expensive attire, fashionable shoes and telephones, to mention but a few." I don't want you steal anything from others "Yes I do mum." "Because maybe those students have rich parents who can afford to provide them. Do have them? "NO," I said. "No, so you don't try to copy any negative behavior from people." She said "**Never Forget You and be you.**"

I convinced her that I will follow the advice she had given me. The main issue from the words of Mama Ange is to enlighten some people who don't consider their individuality and accept to imitate others like in characters. Some students depart from their homes for studies but unfortunately, reaching the school he or she becomes so careless. As a result of that, failure is number one which leads to trampling on his or her future life. A big percentage of people who are living in misery, want to live a lifestyle of others even when they are not of the same caliber. Because you have seen someone buying something, you also immediately develop a burning desire to buy it also and yet you are not of the same potential.

- Many others take drugs or strong alcohol due to peer pressure, while others do expensive parties. After the party what was pleasure becomes a curse due to heavy debts.
- Again, another group falls into debts wanting to buy expensive cars. Be satisfied with the level you are in, that's my advice. Take your time; slowly by slowly an

egg can walk in one day, it takes 21 days. Remember that human being appears only once in life.

– There are some who can't do something to develop themselves, being weakened by their friends, that even if they try, they can't succeed and from there they believe it's true.

My appeal is that, if you want to achieve dreams you set, try to stand on your individuality and never be taken up by characters of others. Never waste time on what people are thinking of about you, ignore them because you're not in their hearts. Learn self-belief, I mean trust yourself. You are of great value compared to others. Don't waste your possessions pretending to be like others and as a result debts and critics may arise. Understand well that it's advisable to imitate good ideas from other people, not bad. Let's study how to maintain our dignity, and focus ahead. Do you dress the way you want to dress? Do you listen to the music you really like, or do you follow others' will? Are you working on your dreams or the dreams of someone else? We like to make a photocopy of others' like shopping, drinking, studies, gossiping smoking, driving, weddings, and business and many more. Just be yourself. You are a powerful person. You have something special, you have greatness within you, you are endowed with talents, ability, skills, you even don't know. If you are looking bad, no problem, ignore that; if you are looking good, it's ok. Perhaps you can call your mom and show her that you are not looking nice and to reproduce you, if possible and become awesome. Just be yourself.

60 Principles of Life Enrichment

1. Live your life as a master piece.
2. Your thoughts define your reality.
3. If you give your heart talk's second position, then you will always be second in life, not first.
4. You have already everything to become successful in true meaning.
5. Your outside prosperity is directly equal to your inner prosperity.
6. Your life is your own responsibility and it's you who matters most in your success.
7. Relationship is everything.
8. How many college degrees you have is one thing, but how much real life education you have, what everything is.
9. You grow as much as your awareness grows about life.
10. You cannot change people, but you definitely change yourself.
11. Your interaction skills with people are your most valuable asset for success.
12. Don't think people are poor, due to lack of money but the reality is that, they are poor in deciding what actually they want in life.
13. Adopt the habit of writing a journal.
14. Understand the deeper meaning of your profession.
15. Find some real reason why you should be successful.
16. Understand completely the law of attraction.
17. Only you can change those things about which you have awareness.

18. Change is always good and it provides opportunities for growth.
19. Start from where you are exactly right now.
20. Love is everything.
21. You cannot overtake your thinking.
22. Don't blame others for your life.
23. Your E.Q. is more important than your I.Q.
24. Define what the actual meaning of success is, for you.
25. Think deeply if no one will dare to do new things, how boring life will be.
26. Don't hesitate; simply ask about what you don't know.
27. Only go to experts for important suggestions.
28. Read again and again success stories of people, who influence you.
29. Make your own library of real and positive books.
30. Make friends from every field because that will increase your interest and enjoyment in life.
31. Always remember that in life you are not alone. God has not given up on you.
32. Get prepared and do not wait for any opportunity to come search for you, go and search for them everywhere. As my Mentor Les Brown said in he is book, "Live Your Dreams" "I believe that opportunities still exist for those who are willing to get in the door and bide their time until openings appear."
33. Focus on your potential, not on your limitations.
34. Always be positive. Never think or speaks negatively about yourself and others in life.

35. Have the hope that even if you're facing challenges in life, remembers that there is happiness too. In the future, the problems you're facing will end.
36. Be aware that your life is precious and that there is no one apart from you, who can change it, but YOU.
37. Don't consider your life as a burden, but rather as a gift from God.
38. Learn to think positively and read books that can help you build your hope, watch films that can maintain your life positively.
39. Always pray and remember that God is greater than your problem.
40. Even when you go through a multitude of hardships in life, you must have goals in your life.
41. When you are in problems, when you see earth is pushing you down, give yourself a time in conversation and think of how to overcome it, because there will be a solution for any kind of problem.
42. You can't be good to others, if you are not good to yourself.
43. The way you value yourself, is the way others value you.
44. Love your life because if you don't, no one will do it for you.
45. Your life and future are in your hands and you are the pilot. Either you drive fast or slow. The choice is yours.
46. If you want to achieve super success in life, give yourself more time to concentrate, by doing what you love the most.

47. The best friend you can have, the one you can trust more during problems, or suffering moments, is only YOU.
48. High commitment will lead you to great achievement.
49. Expect nothing from everything, but better from yourself.
50. Things happen in their own way, but try to do better from your own side.
51. Through the process of change, things can be achieved in a remarkable manner.
52. Be aware that whenever there is a problem, there is a solution. Find the solution. Be aware that whenever a problem is allowed get big, it becomes even bigger and overpower you, if given a chance. When you ignore it, however much or big it would be, it loses the value. That is the better advice.
53. Be aware that problems are not the calendar of your life. The day when they will get over, with the rise of another and what was a problem will turn into joy. Therefore, be firm and don't give up on your dreams or you leave what you started.
54. In life many things happen. There is suffering, losing our beloved ones, losing a job suddenly, failing in school, lack of money to pay fees etc. But the thing you must know the most is that problems are part of life that we must face and deal with.
55. We don't need to have everything, in other to start something. But we must to start something, to get everything we need in life.
56. Speak less, listen more, learn more and grow.

57. When you change the way you see yourself and the way you see things positively, everything will change and your life will change forever.
58. I endured hard times, bad weather, hunger and worked tirelessly with much courage, not because I liked it, but only driven by what I could get after work.
59. We have two options about time in life. Either you invest your time. Or you waste it. The choice is yours.
60. My life change completely the day I find why I live in the date I find my why for living.

Part 4

Major Reason for Self-Awareness

Barriers to Self-Awareness

Talking about barriers to success has been a very interesting topic of many business theories yet, it is not an easy topic to discuss, because barriers to success can have many involuntary causes, which cause many people not to believe in theories on the issue. For example, someone who has started to build a house falls sick before the house is completed, will have to use the money for medication, instead of the house. It will be then very difficult to make him understand that the barrier to the success of completing his house was himself. We are our first barrier to success, not our enemies, bad spirits or poverty, as we like to Pretend. I assume it is hard to understand this as a reader but at the end of this chapter, you will get my point.

"Limitation lives only in our minds. But if we use our imagination, our possibilities become limitless."

- JAMIE PAOLINETTI

"You take your life in your own hands, and what happens? A terrible thing, No one to blame."

- ERICA JONG

i. Ignorance

"Be miserable or motivate yourself; whatever has to be done, it's always your choice."

- OG MANDINO

Many writers have demonstrated that ignorance is on top of all barriers to success and it is true. According to me, an ignorant person is one who does not recognize the potential in him or her. It does not matter whether you are educated or not. The least ignorant is the one, who ignores himself. Let me take an example of children. They may not know how to read and write, but yet they understand very well their hobbies and try to make a career out of them. They are not ignorant as we may think. The kid that dreams to become a teacher will spend his or her playing time trying to make his or her friends, students. Sadly, as we grow up, our minds and negative experiences from grown-ups teach us to give up on our dreams, only because they failed. You will hear some parents telling their children to follow the career that the father failed to finish. Such lectures include, "my son, you have to become a doctor, I need you to follow my footsteps. You have to replace me at the post, or you have to revenge my honor." All these are sayings that young people follow blindly and become ignorant of themselves. How come you accept to work hard on something that you never dreamed of, only because your father has said so and you expect to succeed?

I remember one of my colleagues in university used to hate all business related courses when he was doing Business Studies. He would sweat to understand a very simple topic in management and he failed in simple mathematic problems and got very desperate. One day, he confessed to me that he does not like the career, that he got enrolled in the faculty only because he was to inherit his father's business and his degree in business was his father's only condition. This young man was very desperate as his dream was to become an explorer instead of a businessman. I asked him whether he expected his success to come from his father or him and he said that he would like it, if he brings success to himself, but the fact that his father was the main sponsor, was a problem. I then told him my story to put himself in my place. I did not have a father who imposed on me to sponsor me and I was following my dream and happy about my class results. I am glad that my advice made him understand that he had to follow his dream, at the same time trying not to disappoint his father. He got himself enrolled in an online Geography course, as he went on striving to get a degree in Business.

ii. Negative Assumptions on Ourselves and Positive Assumptions on Others

We tend to think that powerful people around us are more capable than ourselves. We all agree that it is easier to see what someone can achieve, more than what we can do. This makes me remember a story that I read; a father was playing with his kid. He lifted the boy on to a branch of a tree and then he commanded him to jump down. The kid was afraid that he might fall down and get hurt, but his father insisted assuring him that he is going to catch him before he falls. The kid accepted his father's assurance and he jumped. But surprisingly, the father closed his arms and the kid fell down and hurt his knees. Then his father explained that he wanted to see who the kid believed in, himself or the father. Don't put much believe in anyone, not even your father; believe in yourself first, before anyone else.

Negative assumptions on us are as much dangerous as a virus in the body. You can imagine someone in the situation that he wants to achieve something, but begin to see the inconveniences, before the possibilities. Don't let your **"I can't"** come before **"I can."** May be that kid could have prepared himself to try to use his little strength to save his knees, but he looked on his father's strong arms, before concentrating his little leg muscles for the jump.

No matter how small your capital is, you can start a little business, no matter how weak is your body, you can still find something to work on, no matter how miserable you look; there is always something for you, according to your level.

Be aware that those, whom you think have got it all, have their complications too. Your path may even be clearer than theirs. When I was in school, I used to think that classmates who came from rich families were living perfect lives, but things were different. There is one in university, he was married with four children, and he had two elder brothers who took care of all his expenses. One was an in the CIA team of the United States of America, another worked in Israel. To our shock, when we started another term, our colleague did not show up and we were wondering why, before we received a letter from him saying that he was no longer able to pursue his studies because his brother in the US, stopped all sponsorship to him. That incident opened my eyes as I thought the guy was fully secured considering the kind lifestyle he had. I was not happy about his misfortune but instead I learnt a lot from his situation.

iii. Failure to Learn from our Previous Mistakes and Misfortune or Other People's Experiences

The other barrier to success is to fail to learn from our previous mistakes and misfortune or other people's experiences. We may speak of innovation and other new things in our lives, but life issues that we pass through are not at all new in our eyes and minds. The mistake that I commit today has been someone else's experience, or it will serve as an example to someone, somewhere.

We fail to learn from our mistakes or misfortune when we let ourselves get consumed by the grief or anger that comes with such situations, instead of looking deep into the problem to learn a few lessons. Let us return to the example in the beginning of this chapter. The man who failed to finish his house, because he got very sick and spent the rest of the budgeted money for the house, on his medication. Was it for the first time this man was getting sick? Or didn't he seeing people getting sick and spend a lot of money on medication? The answer is no, of course. What did he do to secure himself from health issues before he get sick? Nothing! The failure is to watch things happening to people and we just spend time crying with them or much worse, criticizing them instead of leaning. Our man here could have thought about medical insurance, before planning to build a house. At the beginning, we thought that the barrier to the success of completing this house was sickness, but in reality, we see many people getting very sick but still succeed in whatever they started. I hope that at this level, as a reader you understand that the barrier to this success was the failure to learn from previous events or other people's experiences. Barriers to success are many, but we tend to mistake on some issues which are not basically barriers. Poverty, sickness, disability, illiteracy, misfortune, bad luck, spirits, and many other facts are just pretexts. Success does not mean to go to sleep and wake up with something big in your hands. It is instead to work hard, step by step on what we intend to achieve and accomplish it little by little. There are a number of bad habits that contribute as barriers to success that will be discussed in the next chapter.

Sixteen Reasons for Self-Ignorance

Marilyn Tam once said that, "you make well-meaning resolutions to improve your life but your resolutions fade under the stress of multiple demands on your time and attention. Often times, the resolutions are history before the month is done." He asked himself that "how can we ensure that we actually benefit from the good intentions that we made with such convictions?" He made a resolution to work less and spend more time on his personal life, family and health and from there he took the time to ask himself a few hard questions and then developed the five guidelines to have a happier, healthier and more successful life. This is what we are ultimately after making resolutions that you can manage. You must specify your desired end result and make the goals measurable. For example, instead of saying that you want to lose weight, give yourself a specific time frame for a number of pounds or inches broken down into smaller pieces, so that you have incremental targets broken down to into smaller pieces, so that you have incremental targets to meet. The problem is that sometimes we set higher goals, without focusing on small steps that we have to make, before reaching the ultimate goal and then we cause our own failure. Below are seventeen common reasons why people fail in whatever they do.

i. Being a Know all and a Swellhead

The first weakness in a human being is to pretend to know everything and much worse, to be a self-centered person. Such people think that their ideas are the best; that no one else can think at their level. Such people do not need advice from anyone, even professionals. The danger in this is that relying only on your idea can make you miss the main point of your plan. For example, you need to construct a house and feel like you are the only one to bring ideas to the project. You may choose a plot, choose a design and everything. But without the contribution of engineers to tell you that the plot is in a conducive environment and many facts, your house may be at risk to collapse just after construction.

When you get the foundation wrong, you will continue to make mistakes and be completely unaware that your initial idea was wrong and that it is leading to your failure. My appeal is that those who think that they know all and self-sufficient should start to welcome other people's ideas and become all time learners and teachable to succeed in this life.

ii. Rushing through it without much thought

A majority of people do not have the time to think about what they are going to do. Instead you find them fighting hard so that they may accomplish what they are doing. When you don't spare time to think and think over again on before you start an activity, you risk to make irreversible mistakes. Instead quickly rushing on what you are asked to do only because the task is to finish on time, you risk to restart and use double the time.

"Rushing is a virus in action." The consequence of rushing normally is to make mistakes. It is therefore better to take your time and think of the best way to complete your activity, before you start it, so that you complete it as it was required. The logic here is to slow down never trying to finish everything in one day or in few minutes just that you spare sometime for yourself. Mind about the quality instead of quantity and you will see much improvement in handling tasks. Then efficiency will be the result as well. There is a saying that "you miss to fix the nail where it is supposed to be and then it becomes difficult to pull it out." Execute your thinking capacity and never rush.

iii. Lack of concentration

Research show that many people spend a lot time correcting mistakes done either by others or themselves. Many mistakes are caused by the fact that the activities were done without much concentration. If you are doing something and your mind is away from it, there will be no success. Some errors may occur which sometimes are very difficult to correct. In order to avoid that, you need completely focus on what you are doing and give it full attention.

iv. Allowing frustrations to take advantage

When you are in the middle of an activity, some serious problem may occur to make you frustrated and you start to think that whatever you will be do, will not come out well. This will cause an anguished spirit in you and as the anger continues to grow, the adrenaline will flow ways and around in your body and risk to make you ill. What you need to do is to look for the ways and means of preventing frustration to drive you. You need to calm down by finding time for yourself and relax; and then try to understand that in life, there are ups and downs, so when you develop that heart and become a master of your moods, you will see things becoming easier for you.

v. Forcing ourselves to do something which we have no interest in.

When we try to do something which we find boring and tiresome, the result is that we become quickly exhausted.

You cannot offer to give enough time and energy to bring an activity to the required standards when you do not care. On the contrary, when you do something that you love and have in heart, you will surely do everything that it takes, to see it complete. It is not advisable to start doing something which you dislike or not interested in, because it may become a burden to you, thus bringing you to a total failure. Herbert Harris notes that, "Is there anything about the way you think or feel about yourself that will frustrate your success effort? If so, handle it immediately. Do whatever it takes to become the person you must be, to accomplish your goals and realize your vision."

vi. Procrastination

Procrastination is a bad habit of pushing activities away for some other time. Procrastinators need to be given deadlines for them to complete their activities. What are they going to become when they will be the ones to set the deadlines? Do an activity in its due time, especially when you know that no one else is going to do it for you. Do not wait for the last day to accomplish something that you could have worked on some days back. Procrastination leads to complete failure. Avoid it as much as you can.

vii. Believing in others more than we do in ourselves

Many people trust others more than themselves, and this is lack of self-confidence and it is dangerous. People who do not trust in themselves are always reluctant about activities. They are afraid that they are doing it wrong and need someone to intervene and tell them that they are good to go. The danger here is that you may risk to believe in the wrong person who is going to keep on discouraging you and risk to fail when you were in the right path. Be sure about what you can do and trust yourself, because you are the one who needs to succeed, not that person that you trust so much.

viii. Problems in decision making

Many people are not able to decide for themselves. Some wait for their parents to decide for themselves and others their friends. This is a problem, because when it comes on deciding to change, for example a bad behavior, no one will be able to decide for you. You have to know that you are solely the boss of your life and the planner of your future; program your life, if not, the life will program you with failure in everything that you do.

ix. Not being organized/programmed

When you observe critically, you will find that there are people who do not have a program to follow. You will clearly get the truth about this, when you arrange an appointment with someone at a fixed time, but at the end, the person is going to make you wait some minutes or hours before he or she arrives. But why? The reason is that he or she is not programmed. He or she does not have a daily activity schedule to use. He or she does not know what to do now or then, tomorrow or the day after. Being disorganized is the chief cause of daily bad results in your affairs. You must organize yourself in everything you do.

x. Lack of time to break

Breaks refresh the nerves. You should find time to refresh yourself for better performance. When I was in secondary school, the class was from 8 to 12AM. Then lunch time of one hour before 1 to 4 PM. My daily timetable gave me at least 45 minutes for rest. This helped me for staying focused in the afternoon classes. Some students used the break time to revise or play tiresome games and in the afternoon, they were all sleepy in class. The same advice goes to you. Break hours are special. It is much like recharging our brain batteries.

xi. Lack of sleep

A normal person should sleep for 6 to 8 hours a night. A healthy sleep will help to keep you awake the whole day. Thus perform your work well and you will have enough energy for whatever you do. The ability to think also relates to the way we rest at night. Ignoring all these, leads to poor performance, stress, sickness and then failure. It is better to have enough rest. I have friend who likes to watch football, to the point that he choose to stay awake the whole night, even if there was an exam, the following morning. When we were in secondary school, the guy could even miss his supper meal, because of a football match. The results were that he always looked tired and sleepy and could not perform well in class, unless the premier league was over.

xii. Lack of a daily activity schedule

Many of us do not see the importance of scheduling daily activities. This results in poor time management and confusion about activities. To be more effective in time management, you should prepare yourself by making a list of tasks, to accomplish every day. Sometimes we focus on weekly or monthly activities, forgetting that they must be accomplished through daily activities. If you fail to have a list of things to do in single day, do not expect to succeed with your weekly activities. This also causes people to mix what they planned to do. I remember a friend called Peter. One day he asked me to accompany him to the market as he wanted to buy a radio, but at the end, he found himself buying a TV and other home equipment. This is not good, because he used up the money he had planned, for other things. It is good to have a list of activities, because it keeps us organized. Focus on today's tasks. Do them well. Once today's tasks are completed, prepare tomorrow's tasks. When tomorrow's tasks are complete, work on the other tasks, due by the end of the week, and when those are complete, work on the tasks, due by early next week. This will keep your time managed more efficiently and reduce stress and eliminate probable failure. Don't allow yourself to make unrealistic plans that would be difficult to accomplish, through daily tasks.

xiii. Lack of prayer

Without God, our plans are futile, but with Him and our trust in Him, everything is possible. After setting goals, prayer is necessary so that God intervenes, as he is the one to make them happen. Lack of prayer will be the source of failure. Through God's intervention, there will be a high possibility of the goals to get accomplished, so that we glorify Him. Prayer must be given first priority in each and everything you do. Let us try to understand the privilege of prayers.

- We make a profound attachment with our Lord.
- We get strength to understand the real vision of what we do.
- We get power to get the plans of the evil spirits out of our plans.

- We get a chance of a positive answer from people who can help us after God appeases our hearts.
- It is through prayers that we make our wants known to God.
- It is also to put yourself, your family, your wealth and everything you have, under God's insurance!
- Every problem can be solved well if you pray.
- You receive guidance in problems if you pray.
- Keeping in touch with God all time and always.

xiv. Lack of education

Education is very important to help you, to be who you want to be, in life. The lack of education contributes highly to failure, because when someone is not educated, he or she does not have enough information, on how to go with their plans and their execution. A minimum level of education is required related to the field you choose. In business you need to know to cater for losses, balance sheets, supply and demand etc. What you need is to undergo some training to nourish your understanding, so that you become effective in the work you are going to do. It is my humble prayer that you do not neglect education. Study to the highest level that you can. Education goes hand in hand with learning from experience, because one may be educated, but fail to learn, thus meeting difficulties in fighting against the problems that society brings in. I personably I have got a company in Kigali, but in order for me to succeed in my business affairs, I saw it necessary to continue with my studies up-to the highest level of education (PhD) and now company is progressing as I am applying the skills and competences I am gaining from education. At which level do you want to terminate your studies? Start planning now and do not stop until you finish, because education is a key factor to success.

xv. Lack of perseverance

Life is not all that much easy, there are ups and downs. As I said before, it is all about light and darkness, hot and cold, in and out, fast and slow, right and left, quitter and winner or loser. But in all cases, you need to endure. Do not give up so easily. If you see things not moving the way you expected, you need to persevere. It is true that the road to success most of the times is not smooth. You have to practice perseverance, though it is heavy to the hot tempered heart, but you need to withstand it, even if the situation worsens your nights and days. Why should you give up? I assure you many people passed through the same thing, but with perseverance, they succeeded at the end.

Have you ever read about the John, the apostle, who wrote the Epistles and Revelation? He was determined to preach the crucified and risen Savior and amid terrible persecution, the apostle did much to confirm and strengthen the faith of believers. He stood with his faith and preached as he never did before. They accused him of teaching seditions and the emperor decided to silence his voice by killing him. But the more he and his fellow disciples were persecuted, more people were baptized. He was put in boiling oil, but he came out safer than before. As if that was not enough, the emperor again commanded that John be isolated on the Patmos Island. But from there, he wrote the book of Revelation about the future and became until today. Robert H. Schuller said in his book that, "The history of humanity is a study of peaks and valleys." Life is full of surprises, but let us understand that when endurance and patience have ripened, they bear perseverance to cope with everything, misfortune included.

xvi. Being good at worrying

There is a saying in French, "trop d'attention qu'on a pour le danger fait qu'on y tombe," which means literally that if you give much attention to a danger, it will lead you to fall in it. If you open your mind to worries, of course you will not reach your destination. Instead, you are going to meet the danger that you were afraid of. Close each and every avenue where worries might come out and access your mind. Encourage yourself by facing those challenges which may haunt you in these words. Speak out these words without fear, "you challenge, though you want me, and you are coming in my way, I am not afraid of you, I will never run from you, I will face you instead, I will run with you, if I fail to run I will try to walk as fast as I can and if walking becomes a problem I will flip flap like a frog and if I totally fail I will immediately crawl on my belly and finally even if I stumble, I will stumble forward, but never giving you chance! I'll never be scared of you." We must remember that fear and worry never brought positive results, but instead sickness and lack of confidence. Perhaps you may be worried about your handicaps or being disadvantaged, but that should not stop you from being successful in this life. When you read the story of Helen Keller; she had been deaf, mute, and blind since early childhood but she never worried. With a strong belief and perseverance, she learnt to speak! So amazing were her accomplishments in many fields of life. But the most beautiful thing is how she has been able to encourage and inspire the handicapped. She and her teacher received the Roosevelt medal for "Cooperative Achievement of Unique Character" and for reaching the significance, "her mastery of speech had been called the greatest individual achievement in the history of education." She was known around the whole world and her books were translated into many languages. To sum up, the personality above shows that there can never be any acceptable excuse for failing in this life. Being disabled or not, there is no reason. You can prosper in any field by building your hopes on self-confidence, determination, courage, faith, love, good will, cooperation and planned effort, to reach a worthwhile goal – your life will be the exact product of those thoughts and of your acts which are motivated by them. Never worry. You were not born with a worry habit. You simply acquired it. Cast it out from your mind and you will enjoy the results. As you are getting to the end of these words of wisdom remember the following points and keep them in your heart:

Always try your best.

1. Work according to your timetable.
2. Prioritize your tasks wisely.
3. Reward yourself every time you realize that you achieved a simple goal.
4. Examine yourself wisely and frequently.
5. Have a strong relationship with yourself.
6. Bear self-confidence in everything.
7. Make sure you have a list of things to do.
8. Organize yourself.
9. Do not let anyone discourage you.
10. Never waste time in gambling. Work hard, instead.

Part 5

Achieve Abundance in 9 Easy Steps

Nine Pillars of Achieving Big in Life

I know God did not create us having an aim of leaving us on the earth to suffer. He created us to have a good life with whatever we want.

We are of high value before Him. You are special person, you have greatness within you. Here I say about the gifts God gave you. No one is without a gift. What is right is when we use them well; we achieve what we want in life. It's simple to achieve something in life. If you do not agree, let me give you a piece of advice. If you follow it, you will be among those whom we call successful people.

This advice will give you the direction of life, because people who are just there without any piece of advice that can guide them are in trouble through their lives. Remember that your life is only yours.

Also as in general if you do not get any goals or dreams, no one can give you or do it for you. Keep it in your mind that it is your life and you are the pilot. It can be good if you direct your life, as you know others who did it and they become successful in their life. Giving a direction to your life is when you have to know what you want in life. Giving a direction to your life is when you have to discover your purpose for living. It is put yourself in situation to make something happen no matter why. You will need to work or strive day and night to achieve your goals and dreams.

Work on yourself; develop yourself physically, mentally and intellectually.

Pillar 1: Have Dreams

There is no one who can stand for another. A person passes through the world once. It can be better when you give your life aims and directions. When you wake up early and go somewhere you know, fortunately you will reach there. Many people are poor because of not having goals and dreams in their life, but surely when they happen to do something they can achieve something. There is a famous saying that, "success is by choice not by chance." Therefore, this teaches us that we have to do something, so as to achieve something in life. Research shows that people who don't have a personal definition for success, goals and dreams feel less successful and earn less money but most of the thing, they are less satisfied with their careers and live within their limited potential fields.

Let me keep you posted on the ways of having goals and dreams in your life.

Ask yourself these questions:

How would the earth be if there wasn't any person who thought of discovering fire?

How would the earth be if there wasn't any person who thought to make a car, airplane, bicycle, motorcycle and other things which we use in our everyday life. The computer you use, the watch you are putting on, a house you stay in, a bed you sleep on, medicine to cure different illnesses. All of these are there, because a person or people spared their time more than 10000 hours to make things happen. Sometimes they could fail, but they never lost hope, because their dreams were far bigger than their failures.

See everywhere surrounding you and observe well. There is someone or group of people who have dreams to do things, the way we see them in our daily life.

Everything you see surrounding has its own origin. There were people who thought of them. That's why they're there now. But let me tell you that those who thought of these ideas were not so greater than you. They were not smarter than you, but they have made something to happen through having goals and dreams. In giving directions to their life, they have turned their dreams into reality.

They did what they were supposed to do. Others died and others are still alive.

Research shows that the greater achievers in the world were all passionate dreamers.

What are your dreams and goals in your life?

What do you feel you want to achieve in life?

When you achieve it, can you feel joyous?

I believe that each one of us has some mission in life to accomplish. What mission have you given to your life?

If you don't have dreams or goals do this exercise.

- Get time alone to sit in a secret place.
- Close your eyes, relax in mind, observe that film. What do you see?
- Make visualization.
- Write on a paper, a story of what you saw.
- See yourself at the end. Have a picture in your mind. Remember that a person, to build a house, first makes a

plan, after he writes the plan and then put it in action. Do the same thing.

- May be you want to be a doctor to treat the sick. Imagine the situation of having a crowd of patients gathered, to get your help.
- May be you want to set your own company. Think while seated in your office, you receive phone calls from different places, to honor you, call you a boss, traveling in different country for business issue.
- May be you want to travel across the whole world, sharing your knowledge with different people.
- May you want to get your own home, because you are tired of paying rent.
- May be you want to be an author of a book.
- May be you want to open a shop.
- May be you want to be a musician or company designer. Just think what you want to achieve in your life, after six months, one year, after five or ten years from now. Write on a piece of a paper and make a list. Make sure that what you have written is what you like the most. Never should you think how big your dreams are, instead get a paper and write how you will achieve your dreams.
- What is that dream or goal? Continue the process, get a paper and write what you see that your dream asks you. What kind of action can you take?

What can you do so that you can achieve it? If it was to buy a car after two years, it requires you to start economizing. But how will you save after a month? As those questions, May be studying for different qualifications in a reputed institute? You will be required to do a lot of revisions and reduce some of your other activities. People do not achieve what they should achieve, because they do not take their time and think about it, if you can think it, you can achieve it. Here are some examples:

Remember **Henry Ford's** dream of getting a car for each American household. And now how many Ford cars are there in the world?

Remember **Alexander Graham Bell**, having a dream. Mobile phones are what we use now. What if he did not think about inventing the telephone?

A child of 8 years told his French father that after growing up, he will make a car. He had a dream of making a car in his mind and when he grew up, he made the Peugeot. His name is **Armand Peugeot.**

Thomas Edison had a dream of manufacturing the light bulb. But he failed for 10.000 times, but because of his dream, he didn't give up, until he made things happen.

Ask yourself what if he gave up, we could be in darkness.

Abraham Lincoln when he was still young, no one could imagine that one day, he will become a great person. All used to under estimate.

They used to call him a failure, after he decided to join politics so that if he is empowered, he can try to be senate and he was declared eight times. He tried to run for Congress seven times and he was defeated eight times. He tried to do business, but things did not go well and he was declared a bankrupt. For the second time, he contested for vice presidency but he lost again. He was chased away by from American voters. But he went on to contest president and he won in 1861. All these times he had a habit of not giving up, even though his dream was not yet fulfilled. When your dream is bigger than your failure, you should not give up.

As a child of 11 years, he begged his father to take him to Downing Street (official home of the Prime Minister). After reaching there, he told his father to take a photo of him, standing in front of that house of the Prime Minister. Then he told his father, "one day, I will sit in this house; I will work in this house. One day, I will occupy this residence." His father could not accept the young boy's words. After 30 years, he fulfilled his dream, and became the Prime Minister of Great Britain. His name was **HAROLD WILSON**. "What I believe is that the one who does not have a dream, is poor and not the one who does not have money."

Pillar 2: Visualize Your Dreams

Visualizing is picturing what you want to achieve, before even starting to take action, using the power of imagination; it is not using the physical eyes, but the mind's eyes and inner vision. As we have said, it is the goal setting that can help you get to your dream destination. Suppose you have set your dreams and goals, list down on paper what you want, the next is to visualize it. Now, you are in action, as the wise man said, "What you see is what you are going to have." Know that where there is no vision, people perish. When you read about Nelson Mandela, who was imprisoned for many years, but yet fought for the rights of his fellow people, you will definitely get the clear picture of what it means to visualize what you want.

As Dr David Burn said, "If you don't have a vision for your life, you haven't probably focused to anything." You must have a picture of all that you want out of life. Believe that you will achieve it, see it, feel it, search it and earn it.

Make your visualization in a positive way not in a negative way because the more you visualize the failure, the more it is likely to happen, as most people say, "What you fear may come upon you."

Positive visualization is one source of success which is common to all the greatest master awareness peoples and champions in all the fields. A suitable example is **MuhammadAli**, known as the world famous boxing champion. He has only lost two fights and he still remains as the greatest boxer of all time. He spent more time in exercising and visualizing how he could emerge as a winner. He could see himself in his mind as a winner. He never said in his career that "I am going to be the greatest." He only said, "I am the greatest." Put yourself in a situation of prediction by saying, "am" don't fulfill your externalization.

It keeps you in a dormant state instead. Let me reflect on my own experience as Ben, my passion to be a doctor and an author started when I was in primary school sixth grade.

I tried to study diligently and follow my studies and my mom trained me to be a hard working person. She said when you work hard in life you will never be a poor person. She used to tell me, "To want is to be able." When you desire something you must achieve it.

I observed all that advice and even the time I failed, my mum would advise me not to worry. She would say "Benjamin, do you know why you failed? The next time you will pass. Just make sure you will never repeat the same mistakes you did. Sometimes, I couldn't be excused for not reading the notes, but she would tell me that reading more books is the source of knowledge and for me to pass."

She would always encourage me, saying, "Ben, you can do and achieve everything you want in life." I could not understand what she was saying, even though she did not attend school. But she kept on advising us to always read books, be serious in your studies and take notes in the class. She would be disappointed, if I did not attend school, being absent or doing something which was not allowed to me. I could sometimes feel that I disliked studies, but she would say, "Ben, it is only through schooling, that you can attain a better life, free yourself from poverty and achieve what you want in life. She said Ben do you see those who are rulers, rich and pioneers achieved that through education. Be determined to be a hard worker, do you hear Benjamin?"

I do hear, mom. You will see people studying or doing other things with much vigor and determination. But if they do not perform well, all those things become useless. They may get results which are not pleasing. Therefore, you must aim to go beyond just passing. It becomes much better if the results are excellent. She used to repeat all these words all the time; when I could be seated with her, revising my books. She advised me to be effective in working. Once I stopped going to school, she ask me the reason why I did not want to continue studying. I told her I wanted to help her to support the family, she said if I continue to dislike studying, I will earn little money and which would not be sufficient enough to sustain us. Because of that, I made promise with my Mum, by telling her I will do all my level best to become a successful person in life. From there, I was determined to double my efforts and study very well.

I could reflect upon my father's death and this saddened me, being in his absence at times. I would try my level best to look after the animals at home and look for what to feed them. My mum told me that nothing can be impossible to achieve, as long as you have the will to pursue it.

There was a time she came from church and entered my room, and asked what I was doing. I said nothing. She responded and "Being alive is an opportunity, never lose it by doing nothing, go and look for something to do." I did not take note of what she was saying, but what she meant was that we are not guaranteed of a tomorrow. We work hard, because what others are doing or had once done, we can also achieve it. Thus there is nothing impossible. In spite of the fact that I cherished football, my mother advised me to put it aside and concentrate on my studies, because all others things could not avail without education.

She always visualized. Till now, I fail to understand, why my mother cautioned me not to waste my time watching films as they have many devotees nowadays. Many scholars leave school and cannot pursue their studies and instead waste time on watching television, and they become spoilt by others who have failed to concentrate on their work.

We must understand how to manage our time. There is no difference between us and those people who have prospered and achieved their dreams more than us. They learnt and accepted to only visualize what they desire. (As) my passion to obtain a PhD degree had started when I was young, through visualizing, how would look if I had a PhD at less than 30 years of age? Being an author seemed to look impossible, but now the book you are holding is a living proof.

We can achieve things that appear impossible in life. I used to get close to where doctors were seated. Especially during my study period, even just to converse with them, was a real pleasure. It was a great experience for me and it made a great impact on my life all along. I had a desire to become one of the pioneers in the world, my OB's and OG's can be the witnesses. And now my dream has become reality. How about you? So what are your goals and dreams in life? If I can, so how much can you? I used to visualize how I could be, and now I am enjoying what I had planned 20 years ago. I have used my imagination, my efforts to make things happen. I had implanted it in my head to have a PhD. "I advise you now, take your mental focus on one thing, that you desire to accomplish in your life, see it, seize it emotionally, take action and it will come to pass."

Pillar 3: Have a Mentor

In life, no one can give to others what he himself does not have and his owner is his thoughts, because a person is what he thinks. Life is not like a straight road. For me, I found it like a mountain. Sometimes we climb or we slope down. When we reach down, things become different. We do not get them or there are things which we wish to achieve. We will achieve them through guidance and mentorship from different people. People who have more experience and more knowledge in the same field we want to join. On others hand, there some people who are ready to bring us problems and makes us leave what we had started, telling us that what we are doing has no value. And most the time we have those people in numbers. I believe that after writing your dreams on a piece of paper, do you know that what you need to achieve is not by anyone but it's up-to you. The next step is by looking for somebody who is experienced. Who achieved what you need to achieve. But keep this mind, that person has to be an example and well knowing. You may take his photo if possible and you place that in your bedroom, where you will always see him or her because we become what we see and what we observe. If you do this, you will be helping your brain to think.

I have seen many people seeking counseling and guidance from anyone they meet. Let me put this statement clear. Imagine if you happen to run mad or having another problem in your mind and after you go to see a person who sells hardware or metals to guide you.

I know the decision he or she will give you will not be good unlike going to the doctor who has knowledge and experience in that area. There are some people who guide and give advice to others, but they themselves know less. And those people are everywhere. Do not rush; take time to look for someone who will help you to grow. Personally, I have mentors in academics as PhD holder. I have friends who are doctors and when we are together, we chat about academic issues. If there are some guidelines I can ask them about academics or other topics that do not require much attention.

I am not wise enough to ask them about spiritual issues. Maybe they will guide me, but it is also good to have a spiritual mentor. In business and financial matters, I have peoples who have more experience; if I need any kind of assistance I must to approach them. I feel can also do this.

All successful people also used to have a mentor that is why they have achieved what they wanted in life. Now my question is, who is your mentor? If you have one that is fine, go to him or her, discuss with what you feel to achieve in your life. Do not go with every person's thoughts. Some of them may guide you in a wrong way. It's good to look for those who have experience. A mentor must have a deep and practical knowledge of specialization of the field and up-to-date.

You find in many universities people whom we call mentors, who are not updated and they teach things which were relevant years ago, but you find that are not matching with current affairs. If you want to direct your life well, just have a mentor. Learn from those masters, awareness spreaders, read their biographies, their history, read their books which they wrote in that field and learn new skills. Then, try to apply all you have learnt. After that, you can help others to achieve what they want to achieve. I believe success depends on your choice, but because of being ignorant of some principles towards success, we are somehow very poor.

Pillar 4: Be a Good Communicator

Communication means conveying the thoughts, ideas, opinions and facts of one person to another. In one way or the other, we all are business men. We even have clients, for example if you are a teacher, doctor, advocate, or doing other forms of work, know that you are selling what you have. You have studied for a long time and you paid much or large sums of money so that you can know those things. In general, to achieve something, you have to first sell something. All of us, we have products which we sell; my question is what do you sell? How do you sell it? What are the values of your products?

In order to be a good business person, you have to be a good communicator or a good speaker. Be a good communicator;

communication is the powerful way of achieving what you want. It's a way you use in transmitting information of your thoughts, plans, opinions between you and other people in your life. Because of this rapid development, everywhere in companies, private or public institutions and others, they are looking for a person who is a good speaker; someone who can communicate effectively. I believe that any kind of success will require efficient and effective communication. Research has found that in an organization for achieving success in today's work place is closely tied to the ability of managers to communicate effectively with every person outside and inside of the organization. A manager must be a good communicator. With good communication skills you can achieve what you want. You can anticipate problems, make decisions, coordinate work flow, develop relationships and promote products and services. With good communication skills, you will interact with mentors, you will read books, you will be double your income. Just take time to develop your skills and learn how to communicate effectively.

Pillar 5: Good Relationships

"Tell me your friend, I will tell you who you are." One day, I, Benjamin, returned from school, I reached home late. As soon as I reached home, I found my mum there. She asked me, "Why did you delay? Where did you first pass by?" Mum, I went to play football with my other friends." She asked me, "Who are your friends?" I told her their names; after she told me, "Ben, what did I tell you really? Didn't I tell you to avoid that peer group?.Why don't you hear?.What do you want me to do for you? Those children disobey their parents, they spend the day smoking, drinking alcohol, fighting with whoever they meet, stealing others' properties, not attending school; they don't help their parents, but looting their properties. They are imprisoned daily because of their crimes. If they find you with them having stolen others' properties next time, where do you see me to get fines to pay?

Now, where do you think, I will get money to pay as your fines?. So, tell me why you like going with those prodigal sons?." "Mum, "I have done it today only, but I promise you never to do it again!" She inquired, "Ben, what should make me believe that you will never do it again?," because, when you go with four children who are tobacco smokers, dislike attending school, spend the day stealing instead of producing, poor academic performers and always school dropouts, I truly tell you that you will as well become the fifth, do you hear Ben? Now tell me if you wish to keep a life similar to this one we have right now in?"

"I wake up very early going to look for what can sustain your life with your sisters. I fight so that you can grow. I wish to see you grown, having your own families with better life. I dislike seeing how I spend the day digging for others, paying me seventy five francs daily, breaking me off at 6 PM and you also do all those? I spend sleepless nights, thinking about you, praying to God so as not to starve in hunger.

We eat after sweating. Now, you have started disobeying me, Ben? You do not want to make change for your future? Because I had angered her much, she cried, she went outside and brought a stick, she told me that she was going to beat me. I will leave you having told me that you will never do it again. She told me to lie down, I lay down. Then she said, Ben, you might, even you have begun taking drugs like those children." I denied that but I told mum, "I didn't take but I was given marijuana to taste but I rejected it." She hit me with a slap and I started crying, as she beat me. She would tell me never to move with those children with no parental care. Never!" After some time, I told her, "Mum, forgive me, I will never do it again!" "Tell me, do you agree with me that you will never return home late?" I said, "Yes, I will never be absent myself from school again." "Previously you scored low marks of 55%, promise me that you will improve your score above 70%." I told her that I will do it. "Do promise me that you will never try tasting drugs, beating other children and you get imprisoned."

I said, "I won't do them, mum. Truly believe me!" My mom said, lastly, my son, someone once said, **"tell me your friend, I will tell you who you are."** So, if you want to live a good life different from what we are currently in, you should be careful with people you befriend. After she told me to go and clean myself, remove school uniform, eat and get a jerry can and go to fetch water from the "Kabande," (an area for running water) as we don't have water for domestic chores.

Then I went to clean my hands, got food and immediately went to fetch water. What do I want to show here? When you have a goals, dreams in life, it requires you to have special friends who will help you achieve them, whom you will seek and find, one who whom will be there for you in both good and bad.

I was told by my mum that if one moves with four drunkards, four thieves, four idlers, four poor academic performers, four poor ones, four non-developmental oriented people, four shouters from morning to evening, giving false news of what happened around the world and what didn't happen; spending their day watching television, listening to the radio the whole day, four people who ever regret instead of doing productive work, four drunkards daily as if the brewing companies are going to close the doors, four people without goals and dreams, four home idlers, four people who fear business and starting business fearing to incur losses, you become the fifth too.

Since that time, I begun dropping some friends and choosing others because I could see myself with different results. I was on a battle for achieving my vision by all means; to live a transformed life compared to what I was in. I didn't wish to annoy my mum again. I stopped going with some of the children I used to move with, Sometimes, they would come to pick me from home so that we go loitering or playing football, disturbing others and I could tell them that I have no time, while busy doing domestic work. Sometimes, I could be revising. I had promised my mum to score above 70%. I had to revise well and do everything possible. You should as well do the same, if you're fighting for achieving something in your life. It may be business, education or farming, in whatever you want to achieve in life, you should be careful with your friends and whom you wish to have.

The problem is not their big numbers, what matters is their value. You need to have a friend who will be available in a time of need, who will give you developmental ideas, who will help you achieve your goal, than having some who want to take you back. Some peoples become your friends in happiness, but in grief or in problems, when you seek their help, they give you excuses by their absence.

Some will tell you that there is nothing you can achieve because they as well tried but in vain. They started business and made losses, joined schools and failed. They advise you to ignore what you were doing, because they will not be successful. I wish to tell you that, "all those are telling you lie." What you are required to do is to "change your friend, to change your life." Keep yourself apart from such people. If they call you to join them in unproductive work, tell them you don't have the time. Instead, you are fighting for your success. If you do it once, twice, they will start fearing you, and you will also start developing while they are watching you. They will wish to be like you when it is impossible.

"Changing a bad friend is the source of changing life."

Pillar 6: Keep Healthy For Your Goals

"When health is absent, wisdom cannot reveal itself, art cannot manifest, strength cannot fight, wealth becomes useless, and intelligence cannot be applied."

- HEROPHILOS

Have you ever woke up in the morning and felt more tired than the time when you slept? Have you ever felt your body slowing down your mind and you can't focus on anything that you want to think about? Have you ever felt sleepy the whole day yet you had a long sleep? If yes, we all agree that these kinds of moods make us less productive. Those who work for themselves decide to remain indoors, and those who work for others decide to make up lies that will allow them a day off.

In many cases we run to clinics to check whether something is seriously wrong with our bodies. After many and expensive check-ups, you find that everything is normal. Some private clinics will take advantage of your ignorance and rob your money by recommending that you take further treatment and you risk taking unnecessary medicines that could harm your body for a problem that could have been solved by only you changing your bad habits. Bad habits are reflected through the way you treat your body. For example the way you eat, drink or even dress. However, bad time management like oversleeping, less or over exercising and overworking can also become bad habits.

The quote above shows how important it is, to safeguard your health for better achievement. Good health is source of energy for the body and the brain. Yet, many of us are eating and drinking to weaken our bodies, or to make ourselves disable and even causing death. Fast food that is highly consumed in the world is the main source of dangerous diseases like cancer and heart problems. Our meals should be prepared carefully on a balanced diet to the wellness of our health. You will find some people developing bad habits like eating whatever they get at any time. Some, especially females, are addicted to candies and chocolates that might put them at obesity risk. You will find such people always sleepy at work, thus unfruitful. Eating hours should be observed for a great health.

The same comes true of drinks that we have, daily. When we say dangerous drinks, one might think that we are only referring to alcohol. It is true that alcohol is dangerous to our body, but even sweet drinks like sodas and factory made juices, are. We do need sugar for our energy and the sugar that we get from fruits is enough. About alcohol, only a drunkard can explain how it feels to work under an alcohol influence. Many people have been sacked from their jobs and became miserable, only because they failed to stop taking alcohol. A friend of mine had an interview one day, but instead of preparing for the interview he spent the whole night drinking and in the morning when he looked on his watch, it was already ten and the interview was at eight. He was very sad to miss that interview, but he never learnt a lesson from that misfortune. Alcohol influence is as bad as a venomous snake. Above all, alcohol is the cause of many diseases and accidents. Avoiding alcohol is the biggest achievement that a young person can get.

It's the duty of every one intelligent, regarding the preservation of our health. This is something that is mostly overlooked and as a result, the mind and body become enfeebled, failing to get what we wanted. All good goals we set, thoughts and plans are to be preserved in a healthy body. Many people lose their jobs because of their diseased bodies. Preserving your body in health will reduce expenses on doctors for drugs and times increase your prosperity. Successful people, in most cases are especially those ones who preserve their bodies in perfect health. Having a free diseased body makes one stay live for ages.

The great spiritual book from Ellen G. White (The Ministry of Healing, Paged 309) Says, "Abstemiousness in diet is rewarded with mental and moral vigor it also aids in the control of the passions. Over eating is especially harmful to those who are sluggish in temperament; they should eat sparingly and take plenty of physical exercise. There are men and women of excellent natural ability who do not accomplish half what they might if they would exercise self-control in the denial of appetite." The same author gives an insight on what could improve our health and fitness, by accomplishing our goals, which are:

- Pure air: the power of breathing the morning fresh air nourishes our body with fresh oxygen that makes our body feel good.

- Sunlight: early morning sunlight is beneficial to strengthen our bones, thus makes us strong for activities that requires much energy.
- Abstemiousness: the power of controlling our appetite against unnecessary foods and drinks will keep our body safe from dangerous diseases.
- Rest: getting enough time to relax and sleep is crucial in saving new energy to do a new activity. As Benjamin Franklin said, "Early to bed and early to rise makes a man healthy, wealthy and wise."
- Exercise: our blood needs our body to exercise to make the circulation controlled. Exercise leads to the fitness of our body.
- Water and proper diet: water is the only medicine that our body needs. Drinking water detoxifies our body through urinating and keeps our body fresh. A balanced diet keeps us from malnourishment and obesity.
- Trust in divine power: the creator of our body knows what is best for us. It is by Him that we are able to breathe; trusting that He is capable of making our bodies safe from evil plans is a remedy and an assurance for our good health.

We all agree that our bodies get used to what we make it do repetitively and frequently. Avoiding bad habits is as simple as trying to practice good habits and make our body get used to them. We said before, that life is a journey. Before starting a journey, you need to first see if you are capable or in good health, because failing in the mid of the way, is worse. Sometimes, you may walk in the rain or in heavy sunshine, scorching you, but you need to persevere, even though others can slide back. For you it will be time to increase your speed. That is why our children should grow, seeing us doing what is right for our bodies.

Time and money that we spend on unnecessary grocery or even in hospitals; seeking medical help or to repair what we damaged by ourselves, should be a big regret. Bad habits are another barrier to our success, because they block us from attaining our goal. The seven good health practices proposed by Ellen G. White above should do be our daily routine so that we preserve more energy for our daily work. And for our children to learn and grow up with these good health practices that are going to help them to succeed in life.

According to **Rupal Jain** in her book, **"Learn the Qualities of Leadership,"** there are a few basic health Tips for a balanced mind and soul. She said that experts believe that a 30 minute workout every day and a good balanced nutrition food can help an individual to manage one's health. These tips are:

- Keep a check on your weight. Obesity is dangerous, be aware.
- A man is what he eats. Food is an important part of a balanced diet. Eat whole grain foods.
- Quit smoking. An absolutely NO to tobacco and drugs.
- Practice deep breathing exercises.
- Drink plenty of water every day. It helps us to stay hydrated. Water is good for a healthy skin and other organs. It also helps to reduce acne.
- Avoid eating junk food. Eat plenty of vegetables and fruits. Along with fresh fruits and vegetables one can include nuts, seed, sprouts, salads, juices (without

sugar), health snacks, soups in their diet, as much as possible.

- Practice the age old principle, "Breakfast like a king, lunch like a prince and dine like a Pauper." Keep your food very simple and light.
- Reduce consumption of caffeine, aerated drinks and processed food items.
- Keep a tab on your cholesterol.
- Walk a mile every day. Occasional socializing can be a stress buster.
- At workplace, avoid the use of elevator. Take the stairs, as far as possible.
- Take up any hobby and activity beside your job.
- A good sleep is vital. Early to sleep and early to rise is still applicable, as it surely makes us healthy, wealthy and wise. It also helps to harmonize our mind, body and soul.
- Get regular check-ups done.
- Pamper yourself occasionally.
- Finally, enjoy what you do for your living. Love your job.

Please read the following books:

"Learn the Qualities of Leadership the Leader's way" by Rupal Jain

"How to live in the world and till be happy" by Hugh Prather

Pillar 7: Take Action and Move on Now

I, Benjamin, when was pursuing my PhD at Kampala International University (KIU), I had a course mate, Peter.

He seemed to be very brilliant, because he would always entertain what profited him. One day, he sent word for me to meet him at his hostel. I quickly went straight to his room; reaching there we started a conversation and sharing news, as we had not met for a long time. As the conversation became intense, he told me that he wanted to tell me why he had called me. I told him that I was anxious for the message. "Ben, yesterday I attended a seminar about saving for a better future here, in our university. The entrance fee was a high ten dollars. I paid the fee, for the theme was significant to me. A multitude had attended and everything went on well. I cannot elaborate everything to you. The speaker for the day was a prosperous doctor having a PhD in international business from the Oxford University. I admired him so much. In his speech, he set an example almost reflecting my own experience." Peter bowed his head down before finishing and paused.

I immediately realized that something great happened. I asked him what happened next. "Ben, the man pulled 100 dollars from his pocket and held it up. He thereafter posed a question, 'who wants this dollar?' We were about 600 who had attended the seminar, among which were lecturers, university workers, bank managers, students and many others of different categories. After posing that question, the entire house raised their hands up claiming the dollar and I included. More and more hands went up. He repeated the question, who wants this dollar. It was not until he finished repeating the question, when I started imagining who he would choose, or whether he was just going to waste those dollars for nothing."

I was very anxious to see who was going to be the first to pick up the money. But a majority, including me, were shouting at the top of our voices; me, me, I want it! Out of the blue, a certain young man came running. He was seated directly behind the podium, in front of the speaker.

He said, "I have come, give me the money. Everybody knew that he wasn't going to be given the money. Surprisingly, the speaker handed him the 100 dollar note and thanked him. The lady whom I was seated with told me that, she thought that the man was joking. "If I had known, this man could not have passed me from behind and get the dollar, when I am in the front. On the contrary, I felt shy, as people could see me going in to the front to pick the money." I responded painfully.

"Ben, it was a shocking experience. I am going to summarize for you, the words of the speaker after giving that 100 dollar note to the young man." Because there was much noise in the room, the speaker requested us keep silent and later on said, "Many people sit comfortably expecting certain things to get ready without taking any part or action. They want to achieve in life some things, but they do not take any serious step to start." Some of you, "you want to do business, am I right?" He asked. All said yes, we want. "Some of you want to study more or overcome negative habits like (alcohol, drugs, smoking, etc.), some of you want to increase or gain more knowledge, to mention but a few; but one way or other, you want to achieve something in your life."

But let me tell you all what is more painful. Nobody is determined to make the first step (no action to make things happen). We only sit indolently as if we were waiting for a substitute. More opportunities pass before us daily, but we don't see them. We all want good things but we don't take action to get what we want. We all needed the 100 dollars, but we were unable to make a move. We just looked at it and sat waiting for someone else to come and get it." Finally, he ended by advising us not to be fearful of taking action by bringing some reason like, "what will people say if I do this, or if say this?" He said you are in charge of your lives. After narrating the story, I realized that it was indeed true. However, I asked him the lesson he had learnt and he said, "Firstly, you know I was alcoholic and a smoker. I tried to stop both by all means, but all in vain.

But from now onwards, I have stopped. Secondly, I have always liked to set up a business, but I fear making losses. I also fear losing my job in case my business collapses, because it can be hard for me to get a job again. All this proved to me difficult when after failing, my life becomes worse than the former one. But as I speak now, I am going to change and start my own business, because even those who are already in the system are like me and they are succeeding to make profits.

Lastly, I also feared my workmates. What they will say as I leave my job and if my business collapses?" I said please never worry of what other people may think about you when you are working on your dreams or goals. It's your business, what matters are to have a decision that you are going to make it." The he said, "From now, I am also going to make something happen. I will never focus on what is on other people's minds but am going to focus on myself. That's why I've called you to share with you about the decisions I've taken from the seminar, personally."

I thanked him for his decision he had made and to trust God for the accomplishment of his decisions, "To Want Is To Be Able," I assured him. Peter has now left drinking which was deteriorating his health. He is married with children. He has his own company employing more than thirty workers. The net pay he earns is almost five times the one he earned from his former job. When I met him last two years back, he told me that he found a secret of being successful in life, simply by "Take Action and Move On"

What can We Learn from this Experience

- Today is the right time to do what we ought to do. To do what we want in life, to start with little we have. There is no guarantee for tomorrow. Tomorrow may be too late. Start now, take action now. Remember that some opportunities which were available yesterday are nowhere today and maybe there are some which are here today but will not be available tomorrow. So if you want something in your life go for it today, your time is NOW. **Take action and move on.**
- Many people have told you that some things are hard to achieve, and you have accepted as it is reality. My advice here is that even if it is hard, you do it because good fruits are reaped from a painful tree.

Here, I mean no gain without pain. Take action and move on. The more you do it, the easy it will manifest. You must work hard and develop a strong determination inside yourself.

- When you decide to change your lifestyle, ignore those who gossip about you or what they may think. Only take action and move now.
- FEAR is the number one killer, a virus in life. Fear kills dreams and hopes. Fear kills confidence. Fear closes the opportunities where are presented. The only way

to deal with fear is to do what you're afraid to do. Don't allow fear to take you back and don't be a victim of fear in whatever you are doing right now. Remember that success comes to those who take action and move on.

Pillar 8: Know Your Why

Once when we were in a long vacation in 2004, I was in 'A' level by then (senior five). The government planned to construct road sin our local area, as vehicles were not reaching there. In addition, they were charging a lot of money because the roads were almost impassable. The government wanted to improve the transport by extending a good infrastructure to us.

Again, it was to create job opportunities to the local youth in the area. An advertisement was aired for those who wanted to apply to go and register with the local council.

After hearing this, I went straight forward to the chief, demanding him to register me. He wrote my name and he told me that the work was going to start early morning and that I should report with a hoe to begin work with others.

I woke up at around 6 o'clock and went to a place where the chief had told me to go. I found that my neighbors had reached the place earlier. Everyone was being allocated portions to clear and I was shown my part. It was mandatory to finish your task before going back home. We could work for only 750 RWF (1 USD) a day. It was a blessing to me for having got that job, because it was always hard to get scholastic materials and transport.

I worked for 12 days without missing one. I would toil hard asking our boss to allocate for me a bigger portion, so as to fetch more money and it was so. I would be given two portions; others would leave at a half past nine. I was always leaving at 5 PM.One day while it was raining, I was left alone working. It was evening and it so happened that the person in charge of good governance at the district level, by passed me. They had delayed because they had a meeting, and still it was raining.

On seeing me, he stopped his car and opened the window, "why are you working part time when others have left and in this rain? What is wrong?" He asked me anxiously. I answered, "It's because I want to get more money that is the reason why I decided to work overtime and double the work they have done. As for the rain I don't feel it." Another man who was in the car added, "Don't you see? What he has worked at, is better compared to others." These words fell into my ears.

In fact, I promised my boss to do my work well, so that when I tell him to give me extra work, he accepts it, owing to the trust, he has in me, I convinced them. The he asked again, "What is you occupation then?" I am a student, I've finished senior five, I am going to senior six and I am in holidays. Whatever, I am going to be paid, I am going to buy scholastic materials and get transport to take me back to school, I responded. "When will you leave?" He again asked me.

I said, "I will quit after finishing, even if it comes to 7 PM my task is to finish and go I will never go back without finishing it." He thanked me indeed and wished me nice work.

He set off in his car, but having covered a short distance; he stopped and reversed towards me. He called me and gave me 15000 RWF and ordered me to buy books when the term began. I deeply thanked him. They departed and I was left working, despite the rain. After a while, I finished and left for home.

The next day I woke up very early and found the boss already there. He called and whispered to me that the district official for good governance had told him that I stop to labor with the others on the road. Instead, I was to supervise them to work well on the days they will be working.

When I asked him, how much I was going to be earning, he told me that it was 3500 RWF that was four times my former pay.

To my surprise, I became the boss of almost 400 workers. Our leader then called a meeting, introducing me as the new boss and expected every worker to respect me and to bring all their problems to me.

That's how I got a new job and new salary. I learnt many things for a period of one and a half months, as I was supervising the work. I got more experience from that job. I came to know that people who are more successful have one thing in common, "all know why they do what they do. When you know why you are doing what you are doing, you will make things happen." People became successful and super national or international champions because they rely on "KNOW WHY." That is why some of them spend more hours in learning new skills, in improving themselves.

My question is what is your WHY? When you understand clearly your mighty why, your why for succeeding in life, itself will make a way. The students, business person, football players and all champions who know their why; they make things happen. Be it rain or sunshine, he must to work. He or she does not mind what people may say, instead his or her WHY will cause to wake him or her up early morning for work, to order to achieve her or his goals and dreams. Try to find your WHY, because when you find it, you will be motivated and your Why will take you from one level to another in life.

MY SIMPLE QUESTION IS, WHAT IS YOUR WHY? BECAUSE:

1. When you find why, your why will find a way to make something happen in your life, at whatever cost.
2. When you find your why, the doors will open and opportunities you have never seen will start flowing.
3. People who are ignorant of their WHY, waste time blaming others and even complaining for everything to everyone.
4. People who know their WHY are much confident in whatever they are doing and have power within them to perform well.
5. People who know their WHY make most of their investment in themselves, which is by learning new skills, attending seminars, conferences, workshops for personal development.

"Know your WHY and WHY will find a way"

Pillar 9: Just Be Yourself, Keep Your Originality

There is something I saw in my personal experience. I found out that a human being is created in an amazing and unique way, though there are things we have in common like breathing, having eyes, ears, nerves, and other things. Assuredly, every person has his or her unique abilities (talents and gifts). Believe you have born with natural asset; you have greatness resources within yourselves. It hurts to find people spending their lifetime, no discovering what their talents and gifts are. It hurts how people imitate others, copying how others live, talk, buy expensive vehicles because their friends purchased, the truth is, "when you copy others, you throw away your originality; you kill your original talents, skills and ability to perform any work. You don't become the real original, but the second hand. A certain author quoted, "Be original if you want to remain in the hearts of people for a long time." Truly, believe me! You are the original or final work of God. You can achieve and do anything by using your originality. Just do research to discover the complete potential within you. Remember, live your life and you are the pilot. Always be yourself.

Part 6

Learn from the Masters of Self-Awareness

1. People Who Changed Our Lives

"To know the road ahead, ask those coming back." It is a Chinese proverb. In our daily living, we normally interact with different people, some we befriended and they become valuable to us. Still others, instead of becoming useful, they weaken our efforts. Most of our friends always mock us that we can't achieve anything. Very few are the ones who become like light in the darkness. They give us the direction and create a belief in us, that our future is bright. They play an important role in helping us not to focus on the negative side only, but they become our examples in different fields. To me I can describe them as "heroes." Some are no longer in existence but again there are others who are still alive. I will keep on remembering them as long as I live.

Glory to the Almighty One who directed me to those people of dignity. What I learnt from them transformed my life and the lives of others. I believe even you will bring positive results in your lifestyle. You will open your minds to the unknown. The way you used to see things will definitely change and later on you will develop positive thinking. You will learn practical knowledge through reading on what they wrote or did. I believe it will bring an impact to your own life. I persuade you to develop the culture of reading until you find yourself becoming a pattern of those personalities. To me, I take reading as my hobby, I can manage to read at least four books in a month, but if you will, you can also make it. As Newton Diehl Baker said, "The man who graduates today and stops learning tomorrow is uneducated, the day after."

A Guide to the "Golden Rule Management" by Mary Kay Ash, Founder, Mary Kay Cosmetics

1. **Recognize the value of people**. People are your company's number one asset. When you treat them as you would like to be treated yourself, everyone benefits.
2. **Praise your people to success.** Recognition is the most powerful of all motivators. Even criticism can build confidence, when it's "sandwiched" between layers of praise.
3. **Tear down that** ivory **tower**. Keep all doors open. Be accessible to everyone. Remember that every good manager is also a good listener.
4. **Be a risk taker**. Don't be afraid. Encourage your people to take risks too and allow room for error.
5. **Be sales oriented**. Nothing happens in business until somebody sells something. Be especially sensitive to your customers' needs and desires.
6. Be a **problem solver**. An effective manager knows how to recognize real problems and how to take action to solve them.
7. Create a **stress free workplace**. By eliminating stress factors fear of the boss, unreasonable deadlines, and others you can increase and inspire productivity.
8. Develop and promote people from within. Upward mobility for employees in your company builds loyalty. People give you their best when they know they'll be rewarded.

9. **Keep business in its proper place.** At Mary Kay Cosmetics the order of priorities is faith, family and career. The real key to success is creating an environment where people are encouraged to balance the many aspects of their lives.

Three Keys to Success by S. Truett Cathy, Founder, Chick-Fil-A

I have learnt through more than forty years of business experience these three keys to success that work for all people under every circumstance:

1. **You have to *want* to succeed.** You have to be willing to make a generous commitment of time and energy. When I went into the restaurant business, I lived next door to the place I called the Dwarf House. When I wasn't on the job, I went back to my room to catch a few hours of sleep. One time I worked thirty-six hours at a stretch without even sitting down.
2. **You have to develop *know how.*** Merely putting time and energy into a project isn't enough. You have to study your projected market. You have to develop skills. Prepare yourself physically, mentally and intellectually through formal education.
3. **Finally, you have to *do* it.** Some people prepare themselves by getting a fine education; they come from a good home; they have the right opportunities, but they blow them because they don't put into action what they have learnt.

Please read the following books:

– "How winners do it" by Michael W Mercer

– "Achieving personal success" by Ray Capp

- "Make your dream come true" by Pamala Oslie
- "Think to win" by S Cannavo
- "Why can't I get what I want?" by Charles H Elliott Maureen K Lassen

Keys to Success by Indra Nooyi, CEO of PepsiCo, the world's largest food beverage business

She is placed fourth in the list of the world's top most influential and powerful women by the Forbes magazine. In 2011 the CEO of PepsiCo earned a total compensation of $17 million which included a base salary of $1.6 million, a cash bonus of $2.5 million, pension value and deferred compensation was $3 million. Here are her keys to success:

- There is no limit to what you can do.
- Never let others define the concepts of success for you.
- Aim high and put your heart into it.
- Try to be the best and work to get there. And that's how you fulfill your potential.
- Never stop learning, regardless of one's age, and such should not be restricted to academic knowledge but be supplemented with "street smartness" and being aware of matters and issues in the real world. Keep the natural curiosity to learn something new every day.
- Keep an open mind.
- Give back the community and neighborhood more than what you took out of them.
- Be yourself.
- Never hide what makes you.
- She believes that success is not money, prestige or power because net worth can never define self-worth.

True success is being happy with yourself. And that comes from devoting your time your life to doing what you love the most.

- She once said that the core of concepts of success lies in knowing "what you want to do in life" and those you have triumphed at "figuring out" that issue should consider themselves "tremendously blessed."
- According to her "family, friend and faith" are the central pillars of success. When things look bleak and uncertain, it is your family, friends and faith that pull you through and "when I'm wrestling with change in my life, good or bad, the first place I turn to, is my religion. I tell you it really helps," she believed.

Please read the following books:

- "Goals" by Brian Tracy
- "The greatest secret of all" by Marc Allen
- "Think and grow rich" by Napoleon Hill
- "Million Dollar Habits" by Brian Tracy
- "You were born rich" by Bob Procter
- "Discover your Destiny" by Robin Sharma
- "Success in a state of mind" by Les Brown, Deepak Chopra Mark Victor Hansen
- "Seeds of Greatness" by Dennis Waitley
- "Dare to fail" by Billi Lim
- "The master plan to success" by Napoleon Hill

Seven Steps For Reaching Your Goals By Merrill Douglass Author Of Book Called "Success Secrets." A Common-Sense Guide to Lifelong Achievement

1. **Decide what you want to achieve.** Determine exactly what you want. Be specific. Be sure your goal is measurable, so you can tell when you are making progress. Pick a target date for achieving it. Be sure it is realistically achievable.
2. **Ask yourself why it is important for you to achieve this goal.** How you will benefit from reaching this goal? Knowing WHY you want something raises your level of motivation. The higher your motivation level, the more likely you are to act on your goal. In addition, highly motivated people are more likely to make any sacrifice necessary to reach their goal.
3. **Consider what obstacles, problems or personal shortcomings might block your progress.** List every one you can think of. Some obstacles will be real, others may only imaginary. You must conquer both.
4. **Examine the obstacles one at a time, and think about how you might solve each problem.** Ask others to help you brainstorm for solution.
5. **List people or organizations who could help you achieve your goal.** Decide specifically what you will ask them to do.
6. **Consider what information you need that you don't have now.** Where will you get it? What could you read? Who could you talk to? What seminars could you attend?
7. **Write out a detailed action plan for achieving your goal.** What are the priorities involved? Which tasks must be done first? When will different actions take place? The same author said "*Setting goals is a good step,*

but it is only the beginning. It takes all seven steps to make sure you actually follow through, and by so doing achieve your goal."

Three pieces of advice for a high success in Life from **T.HARV EKER,** author of **"SECRETS OF THE MILLIONAIRE MIND"** recommended by the **New York Times, Wall Street Journal** Commit to your growth. Each month read at least one book, listen to one educational tape or CD, or take a seminar on money, business, or personal development. Your knowledge, your confidence and your success will soar.

1. Consider hiring a personal coach to keep you on track.
2. Attend the Millionaire Mind Intensive. This amazing event has transformed the lives of thousands and thousands of people and will transform your life too.

The 11 Rules for a Deeply Rewarding Life by Robin Sharma

He is the *bestselling author of* **"THE MASTERY MANUAL." A Life-changing Guide for Personal and Professional Greatness** *Place people over possessions.*

1. *Never stop doing what you love.*
2. *Always stay true to yourself.*
3. *Remember that we see the world not as it is but as we are.*
4. *Turn your wounds into wisdom and look for the gifts of your failure.*
5. *Be the kindest person you know.*
6. *Do at least one thing every day makes your palms sweat.*
7. *Read from wisdom literature for at least 30 minutes each day.*
8. *Spend at least one hour in a week in silence and nature to renew yourself.*

9. *Commit to a serious exercise program to awaken your best physical life.*
10. *Dedicate yourself to making your mark and leaving a legacy.*

Four Ways to Develop the Big Thinker's Vocabulary by David Joseph Schwartz Bestseller Author of The Magic of Thinking Big

1. **Use big positive, cheerful words and phrases to describe how you feel.** *When someone asks, "How do you feel today?" and you respond with an "I'm tired. I have a headache. I wish it were Saturday, don't feel so good," you actually make yourself feel worse. Practice this: It is a very simple point, but it has tremendous power. Every time someone asks you "How are you?" or "How are you feeling today?" respond with a "Just wonderful, thanks, and you?" or say "Great" or "Fine." Say you feel wonderful at every possible opportunity and you will begin to feel wonderful and bigger, too. Become known as a person who always feels great. It wins friends.*
2. **Use bright, cheerful, favorable words and phrase to describe other people.** *Make it a rule to have a big positive word for all your friends and associates. When you and someone else are discussing an absent third party, be sure you compliment him with big words and phrase like* ***"he is really a fine fellow."*** *"They tell me he is working out wonderfully well." Be extremely careful to avoid the petty cut-him-down language. Sooner or later third parties hear what's been said, and then such talk only cuts you down.*
3. **Use positive language to encourage others.** *Compliment people personally ate every opportunity. Everyone you know craves praise. Have a special good word for your wife*

or husband every day. Notice and compliment the people who work with you. Praise, sincerely administered, is a success tool. Use it! Use it again and again and again. Compliment people on their appearance, their work, their achievements their families.

4. **Use positive words to outline plans to others.** *When people hear something like this, "Here is some good news. We face a genuine opportunity...," their minds start to sparkle. But when they hear something like "whether we like it or not, we have got a job to do," the mind movie is dull, boring, and they react accordingly. Promise victory and watch eyes light up. Promise victory and win support. Build castles, don't dig graves!*

Six Rules for Getting Unstuck By Les Brown Bestseller, Author of the Book 'Live Your Dreams'

1. *Work harder toward your goals. Just the act of working harder focuses your mind and your actions, pulling you out of lethargy and into becoming an active life force again.*
2. *Be creative and change your approach to life Get those wheels turning. Feel the energy flowing. Look for new ways to solve your problems.*
3. *Modify your goals. A goal galore exists out there. Find one, get on top of it and climb to the next highest.*
4. *Ask for help. Support groups work They tell you that you that you are not alone and they are run by people who often understand exactly where you are coming from where you need to go*
5. *Stay busy. Don't make major decisions if you are depressed or frightened, but keep moving, feel your life force in the motion. You have control.*

6. *Listen to positive music, watches positive videos or movies, and hang out with positive, upbeat people. The last thing a blue mood needs is more blues. Don't be a volunteer victim, be a fighter.*

2. 101 Awesome and Life-Changing Books for You

For your better understanding of your own self in future as well, we are sharing a treasure of valuable books with you. Here, we are presenting a list of 101 books which will make you realize that you are here on a special purpose and your life matters. We really appreciate your in born talents and your ability to turn your dreams into reality. To make our point more permanent, we are taking the help of world class authors who are supporting our belief about your inner infinite creative potential. So the list is with you and you have to decide when you are going to read these life-changing books. We pray to God that when you read them, you realize the awesomeness within you.

1. My Experiments with Truth–M. K. Gandhi
2. Seven Habits of Highly Effective People–Stephan R. Covey
3. Rich Dad Poor Dad–Robert Kiyosaki
4. The Seven Spiritual Laws of Success–Deepak Chopra
5. The Monk Who Sold His Ferrari–Robin Sharma
6. The Greatness Guide 1–Robin Sharma
7. The Greatness Guide 2–Robin Sharma
8. The Greatest Sales Man in the World–Og Mandino
9. The Greatest Miracle in the World–Og Mandino
10. The Secret–Ronda Byrne

11. You Inc.–Burke Hedges
12. Secrets of the Millionaire Mind–T. Harv Eker
13. Creative Visualization–Shakti Gawain
14. 7 Strategies for Wealth & Happiness–Jim Rohn
15. Goals–Brian Tracy
16. Developing the Leader within You–John C Maxwell
17. The Magic of Thinking Big–David Schwartz
18. The Leadership Wisdom–Robin Sharma
19. Who Will Cry When You Die–Robin Sharma
20. The Cash Flow Quadrant–Robert Kiyosaki
21. The Power of Your Subconscious Mind–Dr Joseph Murphy
22. A Better India A Better World–N R Narayana Murthy
23. Indomitable Spirit–A P J Abdul Kalam
24. Stay Hungry Stay Foolish–Rashmi Bansal
25. Living with Honor–Shiv Khera
26. You Can Win–Shiv Khera
27. You Can Sell–Shiv Khera
28. Think and Grow Rich–Napoleon Hill
29. How to Sell Anything to Anybody–Joe Girard
30. How to Win Friends & Influence People–Dale Carnegie
31. The Why of Work–Dave Ulrich
32. 25 Ways to Win With People–John C Maxwell
33. Maximum Achievement–Brian Tracy
34. As A Man Thinketh–James Allen
35. The Leader in Me–Dr Stephan Covey

36. The Greatest Secret of All–Marc Allen
37. Dare to Fail–Billi Lim
38. The Master Plan to Success–Napoleon Hill
39. See You at the Top–Zig Ziglar
40. Better than Good–Zig Ziglar
41. Change Your Thoughts; Change Your Life–Dr Wayne Dyer
42. The Power of Intention–Dr Wayne Dyer
43. Manifest Your Destiny–Dr Wayne Dyer
44. Wisdom of the Ages–Dr Wayne Dyer
45. The Friendship Factor–Allan Loy Mcginnis
46. The Power of Positive Thinking–Norman Vincent Peale
47. Courage and Confidence–Norman Vincent Peale
48. You Can If You Think You Can–Norman Vincent Peale
49. Man's Search for Meaning–Viktor E. Frankl
50. The One Minute Manager–Ken Blanchard
51. The Road Less Traveled–M. Scott Peck
52. The Master Key System–Charles F. Haanel
53. Why Men Don't Listen and Women Can't Red Maps–Allan & Barbara Pease
54. Success through a Positive Mental Attitude–Napoleon Hill & W Clement Stone
55. The Official Guide to Success–Tom Hopkins
56. Good to Great–Jim Collins
57. On Becoming a Leader–Warren Bennis
58. Made In America–Sam Walton
59. The Science of Getting Rich–Wallace D. Wattles

60. Unlimited Power–Antony Robbins
61. The 8th Habit–Stephan Covey
62. Principle Centered Leadership–Stephan Covey
63. Eat That Frog–Brian Tracy
64. Million Dollar Habits–Brian Tracy
65. The 21 Secrets of Self-Made Millionaires–Brian Tracy
66. Creating Affluence–Deepak Chopra
67. The Way of the Wizard–Deepak Chopra
68. The Soul of Leadership–Deepak Chopra
69. Being in Balance–Dr Wayne Dyer
70. Everyday Wisdom–Dr Wayne Dyer
71. Your Ultimate Calling–Dr Wayne Dyer
72. How to Stop Worrying & Start Living–Dale Carnegie
73. The Art of Public Speaking–Dale Carnegie
74. The Leader in You–Dale Carnegie
75. The Attraction Factor–Dr Joe Vitale
76. The Seven Lost Secrets of Success–Dr Joe Vitale
77. The Success Principles–Jack Canfield
78. Chicken Soup for the Soul–Jack Canfield & Mark Victor Hansen
79. Mega Living–Robin Sharma
80. Discover Your Destiny–Robin Sharma
81. You Were Born Rich–Bob Procter
82. It's Not About The Money–Bob Procter
83. Live Your Dreams–Les Brown
84. Success Is a State Of Mind–Les Brown, Deepak Chopra, Mark Victor Hansen

85. Seeds of Greatness–Dennis Waitley
86. Psychology of Winning–Denis Waitley
87. Wealth beyond Reason–Bob Doyle
88. The Strangest Secret–Earl Nightingale
89. Ignited Minds–A P J Abdul Kalam
90. I Am a Voice without A Form–Swami Vivekananda
91. Meditations–Marcus Aurelius
92. How I Raised My Self from Failure to Success in Selling–Frank Bettgar
93. Who Moved My Cheese–Spencer Johnson
94. The 100 Absolutely Unbreakable Laws of Business Success–Brian Tracy
95. Life Is Tremendous–Charlie Tremendous Jones
96. Every Second Counts–Lance Armstrong
97. Tough Times Never Last But Tough People Do–Dr Robert H Schuller
98. The Magic of Believing-Claude Bristol
99. The Present–Spencer Johnson
100. When Everything Changes: Change Everything–Neale Donald Walsch
101. Apple Juice for Success–Deepak Kumar (Now Deepak Burfiwala)

3. The World's Best Mentors for You

Having a mentor is very essential in turning your dreams into realities. You are lucky enough as you are being given a list of world's best mentors from all walks of life. They are always ready to make you a "Better You" by changing your belief system on how life works. They people are very good in giving you the message about your inner greatness. With the continuous help of these life visionaries, you can create history. Here is the list and now the rest work is yours.

1. Dr Stephan Stephen Covey
2. Brian Tracy
3. Dale Carnegie
4. Osho
5. Robin Sharma
6. Tai Lopez
7. Evan Carmichael
8. Jack Canfield
9. Jim Rohn
10. Les Brown
11. Dr APJ. Abdul Kalam
12. Allen Pease
13. William Clement Stone
14. Bob Procter
15. J K Rowling
16. Oprah Winfrey
17. Mother Teresa
18. Ralph Waldo Emerson
19. James Allen
20. Fredrick Nietsche
21. Napoleon Hill
22. Deepak Chopra
23. Ratan Tata
24. Dhirubhai Ambani
25. Rabindranath Tagore

26. Bill Gates
27. Jeff Taylor
28. Richard Branson
29. Ingvar Kompard
30. T. Harv Eker
31. Amitabh Bachchan
32. Amir Khan
33. A R Rahman
34. Mangeshkar
35. N R Narayana Murthy
36. Neale Donald Walsh
37. Bill Bartmann
38. Dave Ulrich
39. Dr Robert Schullar
40. Joe Girard
41. Jack Welch
42. Dr Joe Vitale
43. John C Maxwell
44. Og Mandino
45. Michael Beckwith
46. Norman Vincent Peale
47. Robert Kiyosaki
48. Plato
49. Aristotle
50. Socrates
51. Warren Bennis
52. Zig Zigler
53. Benjamin Franklin

54. John D Rockefeller
55. Abraham Lincoln
56. Warren Buffet
57. Dalai Lama
58. Michael Dell
59. Kiran Majumdar Shaw
60. George Bernard Shaw
61. Steve Jobs
62. Henry Ford
63. James Cameron
64. Martin Luther King
65. Muhammad Ali
66. Nelson Mandela
67. Paulo Coelho
68. Munshi Premchand
69. Rich Devas
70. Sam Walton
71. Antony Robbins
72. Sachin Tendulkar
73. Steve Ballmer
74. Ted Turner
75. Thomas Alva Edison
76. Thomas J Watson
77. Walt Disney
78. Craig Valentine
79. Denis Waitley
80. Earl Nightingale
81. Ruhyo Okawa

82. Ken Blanchard
83. Confucius
84. Lao Tzu
85. Henry David Thoreau
86. William Shakespeare
87. Gauthama Buddha
88. Mary Kay Ash
89. Anita Roddick
90. Orison Swett Marden
91. Ustad Nusrat Fateh Ali Khan
92. Gurdas Maan
93. Sunil Bharti Mittal
94. Bertrand Russel
95. Azim Premji
96. Sanjeev Bhikhchandani
97. Nikesh Arora
98. Mark Victor Hansen
99. Lawrence Ellison
100. Vince Lombardi
101. Eric Butterworth
102. Dr Vijay Govindrajan
103. Mark Zuckerberg
104. Narayan Mittal
105. Bishal Sarkar
106. Ben Carson

Part 7

The Truth about Yourself

You Can Make a Difference

In most circumstances, we live a kind of life where we are always taken as people who cannot achieve anything. This is mainly from our parents' siblings, teachers and friends at school. They reveal to us that even us we cannot gain something. This can be the right time to make difference because what those people tell us are lies. With my person experience I am strongly confidently telling you that everything is possible except when you don't believe it. The only question is to know how and what they require. The answer is only what you have in your hands.

Here are some of the things you can do and change your life. And make incredible things both in your life and job:

- Setting goals and dreams in life, as I said before.
- Determine your priorities.
- Develop your life plan to achieve your dreams and goals in life.
- Read books of successful people so that you can learn from them.
- Have a mentor who will guide you in your success journey
- Be open to learn new skills.
- Read and make research for what you can achieve.

Deepark Kumar in his book said, "Apple juice for success, why only 10% people are rich and happy?" I want to make this point very clear that happiness and wealth is not something that you get by chance. It is purely by choice. I agree with him that in order to be able to achieve something, it depends on your choice. If you accept to go with what you are told and stick to them, that you won't achieve anything, it will be like that. Your prayers will be answered in that way. But you can decide to make different in your life. Most successful peoples were born like that, they make thing happen in positive way, they are not wiser than you and yet they hold PhDs in different fields like Mathematics, Economics, Medicine and others. If it is them, why not you?

Four Things Both Rich and Poor Have In Common

- They have 24 hours like you have.
- They live on this planet as you do.
- They breathe the same air as you do
- They are human beings like you are.

So what question do you have now? That you can say that you lack which is not mentioned above? Even if you lack only one, it cannot be taken as an excuse, because we have so many examples of people who achieved things despite those conditions. You are answerable to what you feel you want to achieve.

Three Things You Must Ask Yourself Before You Die

- Have you ever asked yourself a reason to why students may be studying in the same school, having the same teacher, and even sharing the same class and finally one scores highly while the other scores poorly?

- Have you ever asked yourself as to when two people are working in the same company and one is promoted and other are not, despite the same qualifications, similar tasks but one is highly rewarded other are paid less?
- Have you ever asked yourself the reason why some people are successful and others are hopeless? Let me assist you because I experienced that situation for quite a long time. I did some research and this is what I discovered. The answer is "The only difference between you and successful people lie in their time management, hard work and self-discipline." "He who masters his time masters his life" as said by Milke Murdak.

Keep this in your mind. In life to achieve anything, you need to toil for it. The fruit of blessing is harvested from the tree of toil. Everything will require you some minimum effort to get it. But unfortunately, only a few people are the ones willing to do whatever is required, to get what they want in life. They are the ones we call successful. What is shocking is that they do them when we are observing them.

Example 1

If you are a student and you happen to see your friend with a book going for revision or going for research, well programmed in his affairs, showing much zeal in studies, having set goals in his daily life, temperate in everything, abide by school rules and regulations, know well that all those factors can contribute to his passing if all goes on well. When the results come, you find many people gossiping that maybe it was result luck but it was not by chance, but it was only through fulfilling what was supposed to be done to achieve the set goal.

Example 2

Conversely, so many students are poor time managers.

- They don't utilize their time efficiently, and besides that they don't consult text books or pamphlets concerning their courses. They instead waste time on television, Face book, WhatsApp, gossiping and even complaining to everything. Not just students, but even other people do the same things.
- They are the ones who rarely attend classes and are good at complaining about their teachers.
- They resort majorly to football, cards and are indolence. They are the ones who say that success is only by Luck. But it's only about their time management, hardworking and self-discipline. But most people nowadays are spending their time unprofitably and harvest nothing thereafter. However, a good time manager at whatever cost, has high chances of becoming successful both in life and job.

Example 3

Let's embark on the situation in companies, where one is paid more compared to others.

A good and effective worker:

- Respects the clients and fulfills his tasks.
- Reports to work early and manages time as well
- Report to the managers at the right time and makes sacrifice for others.
- Reports to work earlier and leaves very late, compared to others.

In other words, good and effective workers are more responsible, enthusiastic, have self-respect, promoted and earns a high salary.

How Workers Cheat Time

Once, I had some work somewhere and we were supposed to report at 8 o'clock sharp. But there was one worker whose behavior was usual.

- Every time he would arrive at a half past eight (having wasted 30minutes). Reaching there he would start giving a cock and bull story. Some excuses would be right, but others, only lies.
- Despite the fact that he could come late, he would first read magazines or go for tea (wasting nearly 20minutes). From there, he would go to office and again waste like 15 minutes on starting the computer.
- He would go for a break 15 minutes earlier than the others and return 15 minutes late and leave the work again 15 minutes before others.
- Greeting the work mates and conversing on phone also takes 15 minutes.
- Going to the water fountain or smoking would again consume like 15 minutes.

At last, you would find that he had wasted almost two and a half hours a day. You can imagine the kind of worker, surely what can he achieve?! What is shocking is that such workers are wide spread in many companies. They are thieves because they are paid on top of doing nothing. They waste their time forgetting that people who waste their time also waste their lives. On the other hand, successful people spend their time entirely trying to do different things, by doing research and learning new skills, make investments in themselves, doing everything they come across for becoming effective and productive workers. These are the people who are required. The research found that, If you want to become an expert in any field, you have to allocate 10,000 hours by practice. Now, if I can ask how many hours you spend in improving yourself, learning new skills like communication skills and public speaking?.In the last five months, how many books did you read? In the last year, how many conferences, workshops and seminars did you attend to improve yourself?.The more you have knowledge, the more you can be successful. It is the universal law. So do you want to be a successful person? If answer is yes, don't worry. The book you have right is your map. You can make a change. The advice here is to take 100% responsibly of your life, by improving yourself. You must sow, so as to be able to reap. You need to make a deposit, so that you may withdraw. I appeal to you now, the reader of this book, to make your life different.

The Ultimate Formula for Time Management

In this current generation, the hope of the opportunities to live longer or staying longer is reducing steadily. Research tells us that the aged of nowadays will definitely be staying for 25,550 days (almost 70 years, 613210 hours). Remember as said above, in order to be an expert in your field, you need to spare at least 10,000 hours you can use this period and bring a change in your life in this way. Let do this calculation

- We have **8** hours to work from 9–5 Meaning, we must always be on time for work. We all have equal number of hours. We are not talking of the work to be done at the workplace, but we are only interested in job performance and specifically 8 hours of work.

- We have again **8** hours to rest. Each of us is born with a biological clock which regulates our body's various systems including sleep. If you want to be healthy, you should respect hours of sleep needed by your body. If you want to avoid the harm that fatigue and worry can do to your body, here are some tips:
- Rest before fatigue sets in.
- Do your daily tasks in order of priority.
- If you have a problem, take steps to solve it immediately.
- Be willing to work and do your work happily.
- If you cannot sleep, get up, drink a cup of herbal tea and go back to bed.
- Work six days and rest on seventh day.
- We have free **8** hours. We may invest our time on different things like bathing, hygiene, Face book, visit friends, farm work and gardening, and many activities we become across with in daily basis. All these not only satisfy our need, but also play an important role in preserving our health.
- Finally, we have one or two days for rest. Some go for worshiping, while others do different forms of work. Here, I normally meet people saying that they don't have time to do different things which may profit them. Yet they share everything we have discussed above. So I do ask myself and don't get a solution. We have enough time but we are not conscious about it. Time is valuable natural asset valuable we given, you can make more many, but you cannot make time, when a second went, will never come back. The more you spend your time you are spending your life.

Time-Saving Plan Formula

All depends on time as far as you have goals to achieve. You need to do everything in its own time because saving time leads to double income.

- What happens when you get one hour deducted from those ones you used to sleep and instead sleep for 7 hours? In a period of a year you will have saved **365 hours, 2 hours daily** (**730 hours in a year**).
- In order to save **10,000 hours** when you follow that routine, it will take 1hour or 2 hours in daily basis. You may add on, all depends on you as far as you are after making a change on your life. We all have 86400 seconds, 24 hours a day, you can invest this time by pursuing your dreams. You don't have time to waste by involving in things which are not valuable to you. Spend more time by investing in yourself. These are not one day or two days work. You need not shudder despite the long period.

15 Masters Steps for You to Practice

1. Read at least thirty pages of best seller books, updating you every day.
2. Spend like thirty minutes every day listening to motivational speeches from successful people.
3. Do exercises. The human body needs activity, motion and strength to develop and function properly.
4. Make a list of the tasks you need to accomplish daily, in a right time to get meaningful results.
5. Concentrate on what you are doing. That will help you to save time.

6. Make a schedule for each day, week, month and a year.
7. Be courageous to perform certain objectives. Cherish what you are doing.
8. Make a record of work done, indicating the time taken for easy evaluation when you want to begin a new task.
9. Make an evaluation of things achieved daily.
10. Check if there are changes to adjust, to enable you achieves something.
11. Learn from others how they manage their time.
12. Identify the problem and break it down.
13. Have the desire to improve yourself.
14. Develop a life plan wherever it is a long goal. Plan how to get things done.
15. Be a lifelong learner. Be a student of life.

Part 8

A Year of Absolute Self-Awareness

January 1: Be a person who builds himself every single day.

January 2: Cheat your death by discovering your calling.

January 3: Your calling is the purpose of your existence.

January 4: Your own decision to succeed in life matters most in your success.

January 5: Everyone preaches, but few practice.

January 6: Books are great if they make you simple.

January 7: Choose self-discovery as your leading goal in life.

January 8: Make your thoughts your greatest assets.

January 9: Run your own race to win the race with grace.

January 10: Inner freedom is the truest form of freedom.

January 11: Enlightenment means having complete awareness of your deeper self.

January 12: Serve to soar. Read to lead. Listen to speak.

January 13: Share to prosper. Smile to celebrate. Practice to master.

January 14: A clear purpose in life gifts you absolute prosperity.

January 15: Empower yourself first to empower humanity.

January 16: To get blessed in life connect to your purpose.

January 17: Whatever you do, do it to serve humanity.

January 18: Open minds belong to history makers.

January 19: Think rare things to achieve rare things.

January 20: Opportunity to learn new things is always open to you.

January 21: Big thinkers become great achievers.

January 22: Celebrate your failures to take profit out of them.

January 23: Live a life of meanings.

January 24: Do the work to learn the work.

January 25: Leadership is about taking responsibility of creating meanings by your work.

January 26: Your biggest freedom is freedom to choose your destiny.

January 27: Your destiny is made by your every day's hard work.

January 28: You are the script writer of your destiny.

January 29: Unleash your inner infinite creative power to unleash your destiny.

January 30: Exceptional learners become exceptional earners.

January 31: You must discover your calling to celebrate your life.

February 1: Celebrate the awesomeness within you every single day.

February 2: Creativity explored is creativity celebrated.

February 3: Awesomeness of thoughts is the DNA of awesomeness of lifestyle.

February 4: Mastery is not a level, it is a lifestyle.

February 5: Dedicate yourself to lifelong learning to champion your life.

February 6: Life lived with purpose is life lived in true means.

February 7: You must face your fears to defeat them.

February 8: It is easy to live a challenge free life but it does not have any worth.

February 9: Goals are awesome as they develop you.

February 10: Learn to learn from your mistakes.

February 11: Challenges introduce you to your actual strength.

February 12: Tough roads produce great riders.

February 13: Dare to do beyond that is easy to do.

February 14: The ultimate discovery of life lies in discovering your own self.

February 15: Choose to serve means choose to grow.

February 16: You must count your blessings to increase them.

February 17: Dream daily, exercise daily and learn daily to stay active daily.

February 18: Master your craft to honor your craft.

February 19: To achieve the rare dare to practice the rare.

February 20: You must discover yourself to discover your identity.

February 21: Identity is made while recognition is achieved.

February 22: Leaving the crowd is true bravery.

February 23: To go far in life you must dream of going far.

February 24: Success is about going deeper and deeper within your own self.

February 25: The ultimate form of love is self-love.

February 26: Every day is a beautiful platform to grow your awareness.

February 27: Think of spreading love in this world.

February 28: It is your daily performance that constitutes your destiny.

March 1: Challenge yourself daily to do the extraordinary.

March 2: Nothing is impossible for a lifelong learner.

March 3: To grow your world you must expand your thinking.

March 4: A life significantly lived by you inspires others as well.

March 5: To get better results in life be a better person.

March 6: To succeed in life you must discover a real reason to succeed in life.

March 7: Growth of a single person really does impact the growth of entire humanity.

March 8: Unchain your thinking to unchain your destiny.

March 9: Your wisdom is your ultimate possession.

March 10: Work on your inner self.

March 11: Kindly hesitate in thinking small about your future.

March 12: Great listening gives birth to great speaking.

March 13: Peace comes from inside while people search it outside.

March 14: Focus on the best to get the best.

March 15: Success is a state that you create in your life by your own daily efforts.

March 16: Luck is not found somewhere it is always created by your own daily efforts.

March 17: You can maintain in long term only those things that you acquire through your own efforts.

March 18: Peace that comes from within is eternal.

March 19: Difficulties are the nick name of opportunities.

March 20: Design your life around your passions.

March 21: Self-discipline is a must to succeed in life.

March 22: Aim to fully utilize your inner infinite creative potential lifetime.

March 23: Follow your passion to leave your footprints.

March 24: Struggle gives you strength.

March 25: Inner beauty of you is age free.

March 26: Simplifiers are achievers.

March 27: Bold vision gives you exceptional development.

March 28: Be the one who utilizes his inner creative potential up-to fullest.

March 29: Boldness in attitude comes with clear self-image.

March 30: It is not the idea; it is your hard work on that idea that makes the idea worthy.

March 31: Inner wisdom is freedom.

April 1: Problem is opportunity.

April 2: You have to earn your fortune by hard work.

April 3: Self-realization is the ultimate wisdom.

April 4: To enjoy true happiness in life, start building yourself every day.

April 5: To lead people you have to touch their hearts.

April 6: Without hard work life is really hard.

April 7: Self-education is awareness.

April 8: Without dedication you will have hesitation.

April 9: Decide to live a great life.

April 10: Leave the crowd and make the mark.

April 11: Work passionately to earn smartly.

April 12: You are responsible for every single thing of your life.

April 13: Your habits shape your future.

April 14: When you work, work to learn and serve.

April 15: Be a passionate lifelong learner.

April 16: Deeper the person, simpler his lifestyle.

April 17: A person who is true to himself, can only smiles in true sense.

April 18: See every new day as a new life.

April 19: Commit to excellence in everything you do.

April 20: Habit of traveling. The road less traveled is the habit of champions.

April 21: Embrace change to profit from change.

April 22: Follow your heart.

April 23: If you are serving mankind, you are multiplying your happiness.

April 24: Dedicated servers are happiest people on this earth.

April 25: Seek not the happiness; seek the opportunities to serve mankind.

April 26: Happiness should not be the goal; it should be the only goal.

April 27: Happiness is about finding a real reason to live, serve, shine, prosper and evolve.

April 28: Enlightenment is your birthright.

April 29: Live a life of impact and significance.

April 30: Your role in this world is truly special and unique.

May 1: Leadership is about living a life of legacy.

May 2: Never worry about results but about not giving your hundred percent.

May 3: Follow your conscience.

May 4: Communicate to connect.

May 5: Buddha is within you but you have to take the pain to discover the Buddha within you.

May 6: You become what you convince yourself to become.

May 7: Richness is natural part of your personality but because of your scarcity belief system, you are away to it.

May 8: Education is very dangerous if it is consuming best years of your life and giving you a non-serving attitude towards life.

May 9: Service to society is not a duty but a joyful experience.

May 10: your language is an expression of the world within you.

May 11: More you serve, more you grow.

May 12: Believe in yourself to let others believe in you.

May 13: Happiness is about showing your love by doing loving deeds for humanity.

May 14: Self-discovery is true discovery.

May 15: Cheaper happiness is not lasting while lasting happiness is not cheaper.

May 16: Lasting happiness is open to all but it is not free.

May 17: Your job is your opportunity to present your creative genius every single day.

May 18: Self-victory precedes public victory.

May 19: There is an endless growing ability within you.

May 20: Celebrate your failures to take best life lessons out of them.

May 21: The power to transform your life is totally within you.

May 22: To become a charismatic person you must discover your passion.

May 23: To permanently change your life, change your scarcity mindset into abundance mindset.

May 24: Choose to grow in life to respect the treasure of life.

May 25: Enlightenment means opening of inner eyes.

May 26: Enemy is not a person it is your own attitude that plays the role of an enemy.

May 27: Your worst enemy is your own ignorance towards your inner endless possibilities.

May 28: Inner growth is actual growth.

May 29: Your awareness about life is your actual earning of life.

May 30: Learning is anti-ageing.

May 31: Learning is the art of staying young forever.

June 1: Daily learning is the ritual of self-mastery.

June 2: Imitators never create history.

June 3: No one in this world wants to follow a man who does not follow his heart.

June 4: Everyday life gives you a grand opportunity to live an epic life.

June 5: Anything that helps you in growing your awareness is education.

June 6: Condition yourself every day to live like an unstoppable person.

June 7: Listen to your heart to create history.

June 8: Discover your calling to discover the true wealth of life.

June 9: Discover within you the place where you are full of infinite peace.

June 10: Discover within the place where you are full of infinite prosperity.

June 11: Discover within you the place where you are truly unstoppable.

June 12: Your true inner power is infinite.

June 13: People of vision are called visionary.

June 14: Adversity is opportunity.

June 15: Things that cause you to grow, stretch, improve, learn and prosper are most unique things of your life.

June 16: One must be true to himself to live a fulfilled life.

June 17: Lucky people are not lucky from day first, they made themselves lucky slowly and steadily over years.

June 18: You are the maker of your belief system and destiny.

June 19: Blaming life is losing life.

June 20: Path never ends; it is the person who walks it ends.

June 21: The worst of any experience always gives you best life lesson out of it.

June 22: One must be willing to pay the price of success to enjoy success.

June 23: The choice to become a better person every day is open to everyone.

June 24: You yourself create your fate when you do self-development.

June 25: The world is a platform and you have to learn to utilize this platform.

June 26: The one who is ignorant is destined to suffer most in life.

June 27: You can totally transform your life by transforming your selfish thoughts into selfless one.

June 28: Ignorance is suffering.

June 29: Abundance is naturally realized when one opens his inner eyes.

June 30: Becoming limitless in beliefs is a must to become limitless in actual.

July 1: New paths are always full of new possibilities.

July 2: Miracle is not that happens to you but it is what that happens within you when you go for self-mastery.

July 3: Self-mastery is lasting victory.

July 4: To multiply your prosperity, multiply your serving ability.

July 5: One has to ignore his inner powers to live a life of miseries.

July 6: One can truly turn his troubles into tremendous opportunities.

July 7: Self-education is the permanent solution to all life challenges.

July 8: Ignorance is the problem. Awareness is the solution.

July 9: What you practice for years, impacts you for years.

July 10: Worrying is the best misuse of your creative thinking powers.

July 11: It is not the result but your own efforts to achieve that results that give you joy.

July 12: One's biggest defeat happens when he accepts others advice about his destiny.

July 13: More you know yourself, more you grow.

July 14: Serve to soar. Serve to succeed.

July 15: One becomes weakest when he runs away from taking responsibility of his own life.

July 16: Rewrite your life story as per your bold dreams.

July 17: Honor your intuitions.

July 18: For yourself you are totally fortunate.

July 19: A man is a visionary if he runs his own race.

July 20: Without inner discovery life lived is life wasted.

July 21: Kindly dare to be different from the crowd.

July 22: Your ability to communicate is directly linked to your income, success and happiness.

July 23: If you are alive, you are meant to create history.

July 24: Never say i am weak because you are originally powerful.

July 25: If you control your mind then it acts like a servant but if it controls you then you act like a servant.

July 26: Destiny is the girlfriend of the dedicated.

July 27: Richness is a way of thinking about life.

July 28: Permanent knowledge is knowledge of your own inner self.

July 29: Bigger the ego, little the happiness.

July 30: Be the one who designs his life.

July 31: You must love your work to champion it.

August 1: Follow your heart or follow the crowd. The choice is always yours.

August 2: You have to leave the crowd to become a masterpiece.

August 3: If you are dedicated then you are on the half way itself.

August 4: Every failure is a new beginning for a new story.

August 5: Every new day is a new opportunity to live a better life.

August 6: Your linage shapes your reality.

August 7: If you are not learning new every day then you are dying.

August 8: You are bigger than any problem of your current life.

August 9: Do it today, do it selflessly and do it with full heart to get to greatness.

August 10: Your present problems may stop you temporarily but your bad attitude can stop you permanently.

August 11: Every person on this earth is a masterpiece. August 12: anyone can change his life by changing his thoughts.

August 13: What you can do is totally different from what you do in routine.

August 14: Make your mental health your key asset.

August 15: How you present is much important than how much you present.

August 16: Face your fears or get killed by your fears.

August 17: If you do not know where you are going then you are going nowhere.

August 18: To simplify the puzzle of life discover your passion.

August 19: Your real enemy is the enemy inside.

August 20: The real problem with us is we simply do not know who we are.

August 21: Selling your talent at cheaper price is a deal that is actually costly in long run.

August 22: The best way to better the world is developing you for better.

August 23: Real taste of life is open to all but only the brave ones take it.

August 24: Bitter the experience, better the results.

August 25: Lasting joy is joy of inner self.

August 26: Tough times in your life come to strengthen you from inside.

August 27: Those who know themselves are always happy and fulfilled.

August 28: Whatever you believe about yourself for years becomes your reality.

August 29: The real failure in not trying at all due to the fear of failure.

August 30: There is no delay from destiny; delay is from your side to make your destiny.

August 31: Delay learning and you will delay your growth.

September 1: Harder you work on yourself, luckier you become in life.

September 2: Your fears are not universal fears; they are the result of your ignorance.

September 3: Tough times give you a wakeup call to unleash your unlimited inner potential.

September 4: Youth of mind is youth of age.

September 5: The one who is alive is not weak in any sense.

September 6: Only the one, who is ignoring his own greatness, can dare to ignore yours.

September 7: Those who dared to live on their terms, they really lived.

September 8: Victors enjoy the failure while failure enjoys the victims.

September 9: Success is not a matter of chance; it is purely a matter of choice.

September 10: More you know yourself, less you bother about what others speak of yourself.

September 11: Every new day is a day of new learning for leaders.

September 12: What matters most in life is what you think of yourself.

September 13: Nothing is achieved by those who do nothing.

September 14: First you create your limits then you fight to those limits, it is purely strange.

September 15: Champions believe in less talks, more actions.

September 16: It is not about what you do, it is about why and how you do what you do.

September 17: Limits of your thinking set the limits of your growth.

September 18: Running from your originality is running from making history.

September 19: Without working on right things expecting right results is pure foolishness.

September 20: Worthy people sitting on big chairs have paid heavily for attaining those heights.

September 21: Taking something as an opportunity or obstacle is only a matter of attitude.

September 22: Your future is totally based on your ability to see the future.

September 23: Winners are winners because they have a winning attitude in life.

September 24: You can doubt yourself but cannot doubt him who is within you.

September 25: Every single aspect of your life changes when you change your attitude towards life.

September 26: You play like a victim when you blame others for your results.

September 27: You can only touch the sky by keeping sky touching thoughts in your mind.

September 28: If you believe that you cannot win then there is no way by which you can win.

September 29: Go against the crowd and create history.

September 30: You have to prepare yourself daily to succeed, there is no other way.

October 1: Sitting idle and thinking negative thoughts are the two best qualities of a loser.

October 2: Loser complicates things while simplifies them.

October 3: Productive people do productive things daily that is why they are called productive.

October 4: If you are not building yourself everyday then you are breaking yourself every day.

October 5: The people who don't do self-development daily are destined to fail in life.

October 6: Invest time and money in your personal development.

October 7: Challenges inspire you to see beyond the ordinary.

October 8: Your words create your world.

October 9: The best moment to do the best thing in life is now.

October 10: Actually, there are no limits to your success except what you accept.

October 11: Your future is always attracted by your present actions.

October 12: If you are a human being then success and happiness are your birthright.

October 13: Every rich person knows that anyone can become rich by thinking rich thoughts.

October 14: Every single person is blessed with unique talents and infinite potential.

October 15: Less you care about others opinion as you deep within you.

October 16: Life is amazing if your attitude towards life is amazing.

October 17: The ultimate purpose of life is self-discovery.

October 18: Knowing your true self is the greatest gift that you can have in life.

October 19: Your targets define you.

October 20: Winning in mind happens before winning in real life.

October 21: Gratitude is a great attitude.

October 22: If problems are coming in your way then you are on right way.

October 23: Reading is leading.

October 24: Politeness is the biggest asset of all great people.

October 25: You become really super strong and super active by facing your biggest fears.

October 26: Blaming others for your mistakes is a path that has no endings.

October 27: Outside factors cannot stop you if you are determined from inside.

October 28: If you took birth in a poor family it is your destiny but if you die in a poor family then it will be your decision.

October 29: Listening is learning.

October 30: Where you are today is simply because of yourself.

October 31: To live an epic life you must learn the art of converting setbacks into stepping stones.

November 1: Explore your brain to widen your world.

November 2: Your goals develop you.

November 3: There are no short cuts to a lifelong and significant success.

November 4: If you are not able to find a solution it does not mean that there is no solution at all.

November 5: Excellence is a habit, it is a lifestyle.

November 6: Lasting happiness is the result of your helpfulness to others.

November 7: When you disgrace others talent actually you disgrace yours.

November 8: Cease learning and start dying.

November 9: The ultimate tragedy of life is having no goals to achieve.

November 10: A life full of fears and doubts is a living hell, not a life at all.

November 11: Every new day is brand new platform to learn more and become more as a person.

November 12: Every great opportunity first looks like a great difficulty.

November 13: Believe in yourself because you can move the mountains.

November 14: Daily reading is daily mental strengthening.

November 15: Your attitude is responsible for your current circumstances.

November 16: You have to leave the crowd to listen your inner voice.

November 17: Serve the people to win the people.

November 18: Best speakers speak to express, not to impress.

November 19: If you want to master something, do it daily.

November 20: Do not let others define the validity of your dreams.

November 21: Problems are blessings.

November 22: You deserve to live a life of purpose.

November 23: You are totally capable in living life of your dreams.

November 24: No struggle, no achievement.

November 25: Best minds are always open to learn.

November 26: Respect is not demanded, it is earned.

November 27: Learners live longer.

November 28: Grow yourself by knowing yourself.

November 29: All world class people are passionate, creative and curious.

November 30: Politest people are the strongest people in this world.

December 1: Your friends decide your future, choose them wisely.

December 2: Expand your mind to expand your world.

December 3: No learning, no progress.

December 4: Focus on your daily mental food as it is going to decide your destiny.

December 5: Your world can not be bigger than you.

December 6: Only world class listeners become world class communicators.

December 7: Eliminate passion and purpose from life and hell will be the remained.

December 8: Face the fear to master the fear.

December 9: Self-doubt is the seed of self-destruction.

December 10: It is not the problem but how you choose to view the problem is the actual problem.

December 11: You win the game of life when you turn your passion into profession.

December 12: The harder i work, the healthier i live.

December 13: Learn to earn. Read to lead. Work to serve.

December 14: There are opportunities hidden in every adversity.

December 15: Words you use, define you.

December 16: The one, who becomes successful in a day, stays successful only for a day.

December 17: You get more ears when you speak less.

December 18: Successful is a mindset, not a person.

December 19: Victors grit while victims quit.

December 20: Give more to others to grow more in life.

December 21: Either you control your life or society controls it.

December 22: Whatever is of value in life, you have to discover it through patience and persistence.

December 23: With purpose, life rocks.

December 24: Life; look inside for enlightenment.

December 25: Curiosity attracts creativity.

December 26: The one who is serving humanity is lucky in all means.

December 27: The one who is well-known to himself is free in all means.

December 28: Choose passion over pension to become a brand.

December 29: In the long run only the men of vision get honor.

December 30: The one who follows his heart is free from all bonds.

December 31: Wisdom is hard to find and hardest to lose if once found.

My Message for Youth

My beloved friends, development and national modern economic growth are achieved when the youth gets involved. The youth is the strength of a country than others. These will be possible when the youth engage in productive work find developmental projects to set their goals in life and their families and the country to be developed too. My message is, "let us develop our God given countries to us. Let everybody be eager or integrity of peace and hardworking to identify us wherever we are working from. Let us be mindful of the needy, love work, develop our country and aim at changing our world in a better way than how we found it."

My Message for Parents

Our beloved parents and teachers let the children choose what they like to do and you direct them. Advise them, if you insist on what they should study, "our country will face the challenge of lack of actors, investors, new technologists, good politicians, doctors, PhD holders, lawyers, sportsmen, singers, retailers, brokers, engineers, writers, managers, public speakers, motivational speakers and many more. Let all your sons and daughters learn new knowledge and skills."

Reviews

"There are only a few books that can 'literally' move your life to 'the next level.' Luckily, this book is one of them. If you're looking to grow your success, happiness & prosperity, then do yourself a favour and read this book. Not only I am reading this book, but I am getting bulk copies so I can have my family members & clients read this book. WOW- it's AMAZING."

-Bishal Sarkar, World Authority on Practical Public Speaking and Author of *I Love Public Speaking*

"Fortunately, I have gone through hundreds of motivational books but this book is very different form rest of self-help kind of stuff. The title itself is enlightening and by adopting the powerful principles of book, one can claim his share of success and abundance in his life."

-Mohit Sharma, Motivational Speaker and Author, India

"This book has a profound formula of success and happiness for every person who is ready to take charge of his life."

-Shyamlal Jangra, Former Judge and Ombudsman, Kurukshetra

"Deepak Burfiwala is passionately lightening the lives of people and sharing universal success principles with them. I give my wishes to his team and vision."

-Dr Parmod Mahajan, BVSc, MVSc, PhD (APT)

"The time and energy we spend in knowing everything except our own being, simply does not lead us anywhere.

Know yourself. This awesome book is all about connecting to your pure being. Read this and transform your life permanently."

-Prof (Dr) M P Gupta, Technical Education Consultant

"If a person is really wants to improve himself; he must go through this book at least once."

-Rajat Singh Kharanghar, 1st Year UG Student, IIT, Kanpur